1 THESSALONIANS

Moving Forward in a Backward World

1 THESSALONIANS: Moving Forward in a Backward World

© 2001 by Gene A. Getz and Back to the Bible
All rights reserved. International copyright secured.
No part of this book may be reproduced in any form without permission in writing from the publisher, except in the case of brief quotations embodied in critical articles or reviews.

All Scripture quotations, unless otherwise noted, are taken from the
HOLY BIBLE: NEW INTERNATIONAL VERSION®, copyright © 1973, 1978, 1984 by International Bible Society.
Used by permission of Zondervan Publishing House.
All rights reserved.

All underlining and italicizing of words and phrases in Scripture quotations are added by the authors for emphasis and clarification.

BACK TO THE BIBLE PUBLISHING
P.O. Box 82808
Lincoln, NE 68501

Editors: Rachel Derowitsch, Allen Bean
Cover and interior design: Robert Greuter & Associates
Art and editorial direction: Kim Johnson

For information about language translations, international availability, and licensing for non-English publication, contact Back to the Bible Publishing at the above address.

Additional copies of this book are available from Back to the Bible Publishing. You may order by calling 1-800-759-2425 or through our Web site at www.resources.backtothebible.org.

1 2 3 4 5 6 7 8 9 10 – 06 05 04 03 02 01

ISBN 0-8474-0211-8

Printed in the USA

CONTENTS

Welcome 4

Introduction 5

Lesson 1: Character Counts (1 Thess. 1:1–10) 9

Lesson 2: Building Blocks of Fruitful Ministry (1 Thess. 2:1–16) 21

Lesson 3: "I Get Down" (1 Thess. 2:17–3:13) 33

Lesson 4: The Morality of the Moment (1 Thess. 4:1–12) 45

Lesson 5: Taking a Load Off the Mind (1 Thess. 4:13–18) 57

Lesson 6: Staying Ready, Till Quittin' Time (1 Thess. 5:1–11) 69

Lesson 7: Leadership and Partnership (1 Thess. 5:12–15) 81

Lesson 8: Departing from the Norm (1 Thess. 5:16–28) 93

Notes 105

Small-Group Covenant 106

Welcome to our Bible study time together!

Meet Your Bible Study Leaders

Dr. Gene A. Getz is a pastor, church planter, seminary professor, and author of nearly 50 books, including *The Measure of a Man* and the popular *Men of Character* series. Presently, Gene serves as senior pastor at Fellowship Bible Church North in Plano, Texas, and is director of the Center for Church Renewal. He is also host of the syndicated radio program *Renewal*.

Dr. Tony Beckett is the Associate Bible Teacher for the international ministry Back to the Bible. He has pastored churches in Iowa, Ohio, and Pennsylvania, worked with camp ministries and church leadership councils, and served as an area representative for Baseball Chapel. Dr. Beckett and his wife, Joan, have three daughters.

This study on 1 Thessalonians is another in the *Interacting with God* series. It is our hope and prayer that this approach to Bible study will help you apply God's Word to your daily life.

The *Interacting with God* study guide is intended to do more than teach you basic facts. You still need to know, however, what the Bible says. In order to help with that learning process, each lesson is centered on a passage from 1 Thessalonians. You will learn some names, places, and events, all of which are Bible facts that you should know.

Beyond learning what the Bible says, however, you also need to learn what it means for your life today. Woven throughout each lesson are questions to help you do that. These are "interactive" questions written to help you interact with God.

Interacting with God is essentially thinking through what a Scripture passage means for you today. You listen to or read the text, learn what it says, and then think through how to incorporate its truths in your life every day. If you are working through this guide with a group, you will not only think through but also talk through the meaning of each lesson. The Introduction to Interacting with God will help you understand how to best use this study guide.

In Deuteronomy 31:12 Moses instructed the people to "listen and learn to fear the LORD . . . and follow carefully all the words of [the] law." The sequence in this verse is vital! *Listen.* We must first of all be hearers of God's Word. *Learn.* We must do more than just read or hear the words of Scripture. The lessons it contains must be stored in our memory. *Live.* We must put to use (follow) in our daily lives what we learn.

Listen, learn, and live are all vital elements, but they must be kept in that sequence. Application comes after learning. Learning is the result of listening. Start with listening to what the Bible says, learn its truths, and apply them to your life today.

It is our prayer that this Bible study tool will help you explore the Scriptures and respond to God as you develop your personal relationship with Him. We pray that you will experience God's best as you grow more intimate with Him and discover the joy of being a part of a healthy Body of Christ—your church.

Gene A. Getz

Tony Beckett

Introduction to Interacting with God

Even if you have already studied another *Interacting with God* Bible study workbook, you may want to review the following material. These pages are intended to help you get the most out of your study.

Personal and Small-Group Bible Study

This workbook is one course in a series of Bible study tools developed to help Christians experience a dynamic relationship with God. New courses in this series will be released regularly to help you accomplish two primary goals:

1. To know and understand what God is saying to you in the Bible text studied, bringing you to a deeper, more intimate love relationship with Him.

2. Together with other Christians, to grow in your love for one another and increasingly become a healthy and mature Body of Christ that brings glory to God.

Those goals may sound too high or unattainable to you. Indeed, we're not able to accomplish them in our human abilities. Only God can lead His people in such a way that these two goals can be accomplished in your life and in your church. That's why we will be pointing you through the Bible to the Lord and your relationship with Him. As you interact with Him and His Word, the Holy Spirit will guide you and your group to experience God's best. The coming weeks will be a spiritual adventure as God opens your mind to understand and apply His Word to your life, your family, your church, your community, and your world.

If you're not a Christian, don't stop now. We want to help you come to know more about God, so stay with us. This study will help you understand the kind of love relationship God desires to have with you. We will occasionally ask you to examine your relationship with God, knowing that He will be working in your life to reveal Himself and draw you to His Son, Jesus Christ. Being in a small group with other Christians will give you a chance to see up close the difference God makes in a life.

This *Interacting with God* course can be used as either a personal or group Bible study guide. In this introduction we've included suggestions for using this study, but the material is flexible, so you can adapt it to your situation.

The eight lessons can be covered in eight sessions. We suggest that you (and your group) adopt a pace with which you are comfortable. If some lessons need more time than one group meeting, please allow for that. It may be that at times during the study the Holy Spirit will lead you to slow down and even dwell on a point of significant impact for you or those with whom you are studying.

Self-Paced Bible Study

Each lesson has been divided into three or four parts so you can study it over a period of several days. Since each part includes a study of God's Word and a time for prayer and interacting with God, you may want to use this as your daily devotional guide. The Bible study has several features.

Scripture Reading. In Part 1 of each lesson, you'll be given an assignment to read or listen to a portion of Scripture. It is best to begin your study with reading the key passage listed there.

When studying the Bible, the best place to begin is with reading the Bible! That seems simple enough, but at times people read about the Bible rather than read the Bible itself. Start with the text and then proceed to the lesson itself. Audio versions of the Bible are available at Christian bookstores. You might prefer listening to the passage being read. You might even want to listen to it several times during the course while driving in your car or at some other time. We encourage you to read or listen to all of 1 Thessalonians.

Throughout the workbook, key Scripture texts and, at times, entire passages are provided for you to read. This is to save you time in your study. We know many people don't take time to look up Bible verses that are only referenced. We want you to read God's Word because God uses it to speak to you. The Bible verses are the most important words in this book. As you read verses that are especially meaningful to you, you may want to turn to them in your Bible and underline them for future reference.

Interactives. Woven throughout the lessons are questions and statements intended to help you interact with God. The purpose of these questions is to help you apply the Word of God to your life today. These questions are marked with an arrow ▶. Some will be discussion questions that you can use with a small group. Others will be very personal, not intended for sharing in an open group. There may not be an obvious answer to the question, either. At times you will be instructed to read a section aloud, and at other times you will be encouraged to pause right then to pray 🙏.

Use these interactives to help you take what you have learned and apply it to your life. That is one of the unique strengths of this approach to Bible study. It helps you learn the lesson and think through how to live it. If you just read through this material and don't take time to interact with God, the information will be of little help to you. We don't want you just to know about God; we want you to experience Him in a dynamic and personal relationship. Do not neglect the times for prayer, both as an individual and in a small group. Spending time with Him in prayer will be a key part of your experience.

Main Column and Margin. The primary column for your study is the wide one on the right side of each page. Always start reading and studying in that column. Read through the lesson. It is a good practice to read with a highlighter pen to mark key words, phrases, or sentences.

The left margin will be a place for references. Key texts will be listed there. Occasionally we'll place an important statement or illustration in the margin.

Small-Group Bible Study

A Christian who was a part of the early church in Jerusalem would have had both large-group and small-group experiences. Both Acts 2 and 5 refer to the fact that the believers met together in the temple courts and from house to house.

"Every day they continued to meet together in the temple courts. They broke bread in their homes and ate together with glad and sincere hearts, praising God and enjoying the favor of all the people. And the Lord added to their number daily those who were being saved" (Acts 2:46–47).

"Day after day, in the temple courts and from house to house, they never stopped teaching and proclaiming the good news that Jesus is the Christ" (Acts 5:42).

Worship services in a local church today are large-group experiences like the early church had in the temple courts. The early church's small-group experiences took place in homes. Today, many people are involved in small groups for study of the Word and building relationships with other believers.

Small groups may be called a variety of names and may be structured in a variety of ways. A list of small-group opportunities includes, but is not limited to, Sunday school class, discipleship class, home Bible study group, cell group, midweek Bible study, and men's or women's ministry group.

This study guide is designed to be flexible enough that an individual or study group can use it. It would even work well as a tool for family devotions.

The following are some suggestions for using this guide effectively in a small group.

Leadership. We recommend that each group have a leader and, if possible, a leader apprentice or coleader. The apprentice is learning how to lead and is available to fill in if the leader is unable to attend a meeting. A coleader could be an apprentice or could be another individual who shares the leadership of the group or is the substitute leader when needed.

A leader does not have to be a content expert. Nor does a leader need to have studied through the entire workbook before beginning to lead, either. All members will study the content of this workbook in preparation for the meetings.

Group Size. Since the purpose of the small group is to allow for close relationships between believers, the group can't grow too large without hindering spiritual intimacy. A group that reaches 16-20 in regular attendance is probably ready to multiply.

Leading a Small-Group Meeting

The following suggestions will help the leaders of a small-group Bible study.

Plan how you will use your time. People appreciate knowing that their time will be used wisely, so set in advance your basic schedule. It may be that you will begin with refreshments, move to the study, and conclude with prayer. Some prefer to start the study time first and then allow for refreshments and extended fellowship time after. The Small-Group Meeting guide at the end of each lesson will help you progress through the lesson as a group. It goes through the same basic steps each week, though you can deviate from it to meet the needs of your group.

Work at building relationships. One of the joys of being a disciple is fellowship with others. Be sure that all members are introduced by name to the group. Any visitors or new members should be welcomed. Sharing some basic information, such as place of employment or special interests, can help people get to know one another.

Commit to the small group. Some people find it a special blessing or benefit to have a formal group covenant. One is included in this book. It is a way of saying, "Count on me." It also means that the group is saying, "We will be there for you." If someone is missing, make contact with him or her. Do not assume the reason for the absence. You may be able to help with a problem that kept that person from attending. Also, you may become aware of a need. Perhaps God will enable the group to minister to that person at that time.

How to Use the Small-Group Meeting Guides

At the end of each chapter you will find a page to assist the leader(s) of the group. It outlines the basic format for each small-group meeting. Feel free to adjust the format to best fit your group. If you need to take more than one session together to work on a lesson, then allow the extra time. Do not rush just to complete the book in eight weeks. Take the time needed to learn the lessons God has for you.

The first two activities in the meeting guides are fellowship-oriented. Begin with prayer and then work on building your relationships with one another.

The Reviewing the Lesson section is important. It will help you go back through the text of this workbook. It is vital for each member of the group to have the passage from the Bible clearly in mind. While we are eager to see how the lesson applies to our lives, we must begin with the Word. Once that is clearly in mind, we can then move on to application.

The next part of the guide is Applying the Truths to Life. This is where the leader is most involved in shaping the time with the group. Look over the interactive questions. Time will probably not allow for your group to discuss all of them. Encourage the group members to work through all the interactives during the week. Then, during your time together, choose ones you think are most appropriate to discuss together.

Finally, use your time together to build fellowship and reach out to others. Specific suggestions are given in each lesson for activities that will enable this. Sharing refreshments at the beginning or end of your meeting can aid in the building of relationships. Encourage everyone to contribute in this aspect of your group fellowship. This will help keep the provision and preparation of food from being a burden to one and allow every member to feel that they have a part in the group.

Back to the Bible Resources

Back to the Bible began in 1939 primarily as a radio Bible-teaching ministry. To continue leading people into a dynamic relationship with God, the ministry has expanded to include the publication of resources for use with small groups. These small-group Bible studies are being developed as a service to the local church to help you experience the full dimensions of being a healthy Body of Christ.

Workbooks should be available through your local Christian bookstore. Any bookstore, however, can carry them. If you don't have a Christian bookstore, work with a local bookseller to stock the books for you and other Christians in your area. They can use the ISBN information on the back of this workbook to order them. If they should have difficulty, encourage them to contact Back to the Bible Publishing at 1-888-559-7878. Since you will need larger-than-normal quantities, place your order several weeks in advance of your planned starting time. If you prefer, you may order directly from Back to the Bible by calling 1-800-759-2425 or by visiting our Web site (www.resources.backtothebible.org). There you also can learn about other available resources and of new products to be released soon.

LESSON 1

Character Counts

1 Thessalonians 1:1–10

The 21st century arrived with both fanfare and apprehension. In preparation, island nations in the South Pacific competed for the claim to be the first place to welcome the new millennium, and party-goers around the world planned special activities to mark the occasion. Festivities and fireworks climaxed in location after location as the numbers on the countdown clocks announced that the old was gone and the new had come.

And the clocks kept running, the planes kept flying, the utility companies kept working, and the computers kept functioning. The next morning the sun dawned as it had the century before, sweeping away the darkness of the night and the doomsayers' prognostications of a year 2000 (Y2K) meltdown. The world had survived once again. Soon normalcy returned. Alarm clocks reminded us that it was time to get ready for work, and the pattern of day-to-day existence continued.

In dramatic fashion, the calendar had changed. Similarly, but perhaps not so obviously, so had our culture. The cultural shift was not as time specific as the change of date, but it marked a more significant passing from the old to the new. Today we not only live in the 21st century, but culturally we live in a postmodern world, one in which, as Vaclav Havel has stated, "Everything is possible and almost nothing is certain." [1]

How then do we live, and how does the church minister, in a world "that hums with the supernatural but is absent of God, is filled with opportunity but lacks any inherent meaning, replaces responsibility to others with an ethic of self-fulfillment, and rejects reason in favor of intuition and feelings as its final authority"? [2]

Those questions beg to be answered, as do these:

> What does God intend the church to be?
> Why does it exist in this world?
> What is vital and dynamic Christianity?
> What is the true measure of a church?

These questions should drive us to the Scriptures for a look at the New Testament churches. What were they like? What made them strong and dynamic? What made them weak and anemic?

▶ **1. Read Acts 2:42–47 in the margin. List the basic activities and characteristics of the church in Jerusalem.**

_____

_____

_____

Compare your list with your experiences in church today. Which best describes how the two churches compare?

☐ identical twins   ☐ fraternal twins   ☐ same family

☐ distantly related, maybe   ☐ from another planet

▶ **2. Which of the activities and characteristics you listed do you think is strongest in your church? With which do you have a strong desire to be involved?**

_____

_____

_____

> **Acts 2:42–47**
>
> "They devoted themselves to the apostles' teaching and to the fellowship, to the breaking of bread and to prayer. Everyone was filled with awe, and many wonders and miraculous signs were done by the apostles. All the believers were together and had everything in common. Selling their possessions and goods, they gave to anyone as he had need. Every day they continued to meet together in the temple courts. They broke bread in their homes and ate together with glad and sincere hearts, praising God and enjoying the favor of all the people. And the Lord added to their number daily those who were being saved."

One church that helps us discover answers to some of these tough questions is the church in Thessalonica. The city itself was a thriving commercial town located on a trade route in Macedonia. Here, Paul and his fellow missionaries, Silas and Timothy, founded the church that was destined to be one of the most talked-about churches in the New Testament world. Born in the middle of persecution, it gloriously thrived in spite of those who tried to destroy it.

Christianity would one day become the dominant worldview, but that was much later. So in the Thessalonian church we find a similarity with our situation. That church existed in a world that would move toward a Christian worldview. We minister in a world that has moved away from it. No comfort is found for either church in the prevailing culture. From a church seeking to sail against the prevailing winds of its day, the church today can learn to face the future. Just as the person standing on the deck of a boat can feel the direction of the wind, so we can sense the direction of our world. It is not moving forward but backward, away from the ideal of God to that which appeals to man. The Christ follower and the Church need to move forward in this backward-moving world.

Lesson 1: Character Counts

▶ 3. What are some specific examples of how the world and the church are heading in opposite directions (i.e., beliefs, morals, attitudes)?

_____

_____

_____

PART 1: Interacting with the Scripture

Reading/Hearing God's Word

▶ 4. Using your Bible, read or listen to the passage of Scripture listed in the margin. As you begin, ask God to speak to you through His Word. Watch for verses or ideas that are especially meaningful to you today. Once you finish, check the box indicating that you have read the passage.

Meditating on God's Word

▶ 5. Write a brief summary of a meaningful verse or idea you noticed.

_____

_____

_____

Memorizing God's Word

▶ 6. During the time you are studying this lesson, commit to memory 1 Thessalonians 1:3. Memorizing this key verse will help you remember the important points of this lesson.

Understanding God's Word

▶ 7. Read again the focal passage for this week's lesson (1 Thess. 1:2–3) in the margin. Underline any key phrases or ideas that seem especially meaningful to you.

▶ 8. Look back through these verses. Circle one of the underlined phrases or words that you would like to understand or experience more fully.

Read or Listen to:

☐ 1 Thessalonians 1:1–10

1 Thessalonians 1:2–3

²"We always thank God for all of you, mentioning you in our prayers. ³We continually remember before our God and Father your work produced by faith, your labor prompted by love, and your endurance inspired by hope in our Lord Jesus Christ."

Looking through the Scripture to God

Now pause to pray. "Your Word is eternal, O Lord. It is timeless. It is the truth for every generation, including this one. Help me learn from it how to live in and how to carry Your truth to this postmodern world. I want to face the future now with the certainty that comes from knowing You and Your Word."

PART 2: The Characteristics of a Model Church (1:3)

It has been said, "If you find the perfect church, don't join it because you'll ruin it." We should want our church to be perfect, but it will have its flaws. After all, it is our church—that means we are in it, and since we are not perfect, neither will our church be. If no one else messes it up, we will. Since no one is perfect, we all contribute to the mess. Hopeless? No, but let's get realistic.

God wants us to strive to be the kind of church He expects. He measures a successful church by a standard that may be different than ours. What we consider to be perfect might be far removed from what God's goal is for the church as it exists today. An architect might think in terms of the facility itself. An administrator might evaluate a church on the basis of the efficiency and effectiveness of the organization. An educator might examine the curriculum and staff of the teaching ministries of the church.

Here, then, is the realism we need. Instead of striving to be a "perfect" church, we need to look at what God calls a model church and emulate it. Churches deemed "successful" are imitated. Instead of focusing on a current model, look instead to one that Paul held up as a model church. When Paul wrote and commended the church in Thessalonica as a model church, he did so on the basis of its people. His emphasis was not on facilities, organizational structure, or curriculum, but people.

It was to this group of people, the church in Thessalonica, that Paul sent his greeting (v. 1) and for whom he expressed his continual thankfulness (v. 2). Having done that, he then described the characteristics of this church, all of which were possible only as the people carried on ministry. He was thankful for their work produced by faith, their labor prompted by love, and their endurance inspired by hope in our Lord Jesus Christ.

We need not look far in the New Testament letters to see that faith, hope, and love are the three traits Paul mentioned when describing a mature church. When Paul wrote to churches he was pleased with, he frequently began his letters by thanking God for these three qualities (for example, see Colossians 1:3–5 in the margin). When writing to the Thessalonians he was more descriptive than usual. He actually used words demonstrating that these qualities are measurable.

Colossians 1:3–5

"We always thank God, the Father of our Lord Jesus Christ, when we pray for you, because we have heard of your faith in Christ Jesus and of the love you have for all the saints—the faith and love that spring from the hope that is stored up for you in heaven and that you have already heard about in the word of truth, the gospel."

LESSON 1: CHARACTER COUNTS 13

> **Ephesians 1:15–16, 18**
>
> "For this reason, ever since I heard about your faith in the Lord Jesus and your love for all the saints, I have not stopped giving thanks for you, remembering you in my prayers. . . . I pray also that the eyes of your heart may be enlightened in order that you may know the hope to which he has called you, the riches of his glorious inheritance in the saints."
>
> **Colossians 1:3–5**
>
> "We always thank God, the Father of our Lord Jesus Christ, when we pray for you, because we have heard of your faith in Christ Jesus and of the love you have for all the saints—the faith and love that spring from the hope that is stored up for you in heaven and that you have already heard about in the word of truth, the gospel."
>
> **2 Thessalonians 1:3**
>
> "We ought always to thank God for you, brothers, and rightly so, because your faith is growing more and more, and the love every one of you has for each other is increasing."

▶ **9. Find the words *faith, hope,* and *love* in these passages: Ephesians 1:15–16, 18; Colossians 1:3–5; 2 Thessalonians 1:3; and Philippians 1:4–5 (in the margin of this page and the next). Each passage will not have all three. Why do you think Paul mentioned these three qualities so often?**

_____

_____

_____

Work Produced by Faith

A person's faith is measured by his work. Paul wrote to the church in Ephesus that we are justified by faith and our faith produces work (Eph. 2:8–10). Faith is not based on naiveté, but it does involve trusting God for what may seem an impossibility. This is not wishful thinking but a firm confidence. The word translated "work" indicates that it is the end product of this faith. The Thessalonians had a faith that produced work.

The late Richard Halverson, who was chaplain of the U.S. Senate, called on believers to make a clear distinction between "church work" and "the work of the church." Commenting on that, Gary Demarest writes, "Church work, too often, becomes a matter of seemingly endless committee meetings preoccupied with maintaining the movement of wheels within wheels without producing genuinely meaningful ministry to people in need."[3]

The church at Thessalonica had a faith that produced work, the right kind of work—the work of the church.

▶ **10. Think "backwards" for a moment. List some of the work done by people in your church. How did their faith produce that work? Then think about what you do. Do you do it just because you are supposed to or because of your faith?**

_____

_____

_____

Labor Prompted by Love

Love is an action word. It involves far more than feelings and compassion. It, too, is measurable in a church. In the New Testament more is said about love than about any other quality. This is why Paul said to the Corinthians, "And now these three remain: faith, hope and love. But the greatest of these is love" (1 Cor. 13:13).

The love of the people in this church kept them going. Notice the change in terms in verse 3, from work to labor. No longer is Paul talking about their works. Now he is speaking of how they would keep going, not stopping with ordinary effort, but going the second mile and even beyond for the sake of another. Their love prompted that kind of extraordinary effort.

To see the difference between work and labor, look at Revelation 14:13. Both of these words are found in that verse, which tells us that the saints will rest from their "labors" but that their "works" ("deeds" in the NIV) will follow them into heaven. One day the weariness of labor will be past, but the fruit of that labor, our works, will remain. The Thessalonian church not only worked but continued working well into the state of exhaustion at times. Paul was thankful for the labor prompted by their love.

> **Philippians 1:4–5**
>
> "In all my prayers for all of you, I always pray with joy because of your partnership in the gospel from the first day until now."
>
> **Ephesians 4:2, 16**
>
> "Be completely humble and gentle; be patient, bearing with one another in love. . . .
>
> "From him the whole body, joined and held together by every supporting ligament, grows and builds itself up in love, as each part does its work."
>
> **Galatians 5:13**
>
> "You, my brothers, were called to be free. But do not use your freedom to indulge the sinful nature; rather, serve one another in love."
>
> **1 Peter 4:8**
>
> "Above all, love each other deeply, because love covers over a multitude of sins."

▶ **11. What are some of the things love should prompt us to do according to these verses: Ephesians 4:2, 16; Galatians 5:13; and 1 Peter 4:8 (in the margin)?**

_____

_____

_____

▶ **12. Read aloud 1 Corinthians 13. Where you see the word *love*, insert your name instead. If you are doing this in a group, let each read a verse in turn, inserting their own name. How does this affect you?**

_____

_____

_____

Endurance Inspired by Hope

Hope indicates stability. It is reflected in a body of believers who are not "blown here and there by every wind of teaching" (Eph. 4:14). It enabled Paul to face persecution and even death. It also enabled the Thessalonians to face persecution undaunted. And it enables Christians everywhere to face the difficulties of life, knowing that Jesus Christ will never leave them nor forsake them. Though life may bring changes and challenges, hope perseveres and endures in the lives of mature Christians.

Hope has a profound effect on us. If our hope is fixed on God, we are able to hold on, to endure, through any circumstance. The endurance of which Paul wrote is an active and energetic resistance. We hope; therefore, we remain under the pressure and push back with an aggressive and courageous effort. Hard times will come, but they can be endured with a spirit of persistent zeal that rules out discouragement and goes forward. The hope we have in God is the incentive needed for this kind of endurance. Hope inspires us to endure. Paul was thankful that this church had the kind of endurance inspired by hope.

▶ **13. Do you have a special verse that encourages you? If so, write it here and share it with the group. If not, bookmark this page. When you find an encouraging verse, come back and write it in. Start looking! You will find encouraging verses.**

_____

_____

_____

Paul had seen these three qualities in them. Their work of faith was evidenced when they turned to God from idols (v. 9). They served the living God, which was their labor of love (v. 9). And in patient endurance inspired by hope, they waited for Christ to return (v. 10). These three virtues—faith, hope, and love—should mark every Christian and every church. If a church is to be like the model church of Thessalonica, it must manifest these characteristics.

To ask what the Thessalonian people were like would probably result in answers that are too shallow or superficial. Instead, we need to try to understand their character, which is what a person truly is. In verse 3 we saw the characteristics of these believers. Now we can surmise their character.

PART 3: The Character of a Model Church (1:4–10)

Characteristics come from character. What we are on the outside is a reflection of what we are on in the inside. Paul describes in three brief phrases the outstanding characteristics of this model church in Thessalonica and then proceeds to tell us about the character of the believers in this church. What he describes was the result of what they were, and these were not just personal qualities. They were the marks of maturity within this group of believers. The truth is that personal faith and hope and love cannot be manifested effectively apart from involvement with others. This indivisibility is the uniqueness of the Body of Jesus Christ. The sum of its parts gives the church power and dynamic visibility in the world.

▶ 14. Are you a vital part of a local fellowship of Christians? You need to be! That is God's will. If not, what steps do you need to begin taking today? Perhaps they include reconciling with others, forgiving some and asking for forgiveness for others, or setting the alarm clock so you get up in time for church.

If our desire is to be a part of a model church, then our focus must turn to the character of the people of our church. We must first examine ourselves, and then focus on developing corporate character. Paul's description of key elements of the character of this church will help us sharpen our efforts to be the kind of people God wants us to be so that we will be the kind of church God wants us to be.

Evidence of Salvation (vv. 4–5, 9)

When Paul wrote this letter, he was very confident about what had happened in the city of Thessalonica. "For we know, brothers loved by God, that he has chosen you" (v. 4). There was no question in the minds of Paul, Silas, or Timothy that these people had experienced true conversion to Jesus Christ.

This was evidenced by the fact that the Holy Spirit worked in their midst in such a way that they were not only a "called-out group" (v. 1) but a "converted" people (v. 9). The word translated "church" means "called out." God had called them out of the world unto Himself. And they had changed! Specifically, they had turned from sin, from idols, to serve the living and true God (v. 9). This was a drastic change. Make no mistake: it was not just an addition, an adding of Christianity to their religious views, but an addition and a subtraction. They had added Christianity but subtracted the idols.

Some people want to see Christianity as one of many acceptable options for belief. Others try to mix elements of Christianity with other religious viewpoints. Nowhere does the Bible allow for this. As we read the accounts of the kings in the Old Testament, one of the common condemnations was their willingness to allow other forms of worship to remain in the land. God describes Himself in Exodus 20:4 as "a jealous God" and commands that His people are to remember that He is the Lord their God, there are to be no other gods before him, and no idols are to be made either.

▶ 15. If you became a Christian as an adult, perhaps you needed to remove other beliefs from your life and replace them with complete faith in God. Are you clinging to any other "idols" that need to be removed or beliefs that are not based on the Word of God? Take a moment for quiet prayer, asking God to help you see if there are.

Lesson 1: Character Counts

Even this example in 1 Thessalonians speaks against that idea, which was so prevalent then and which continues today. Paul cites their change as evidence of salvation, a change that came about in spite of severe suffering (v. 6). And it was a change that not only moved them from worshiping idols to worshiping God but also transformed their lives. They became imitators of Paul, Silas, and Timothy and also the Lord (v. 6). They grew to become a "model to all the believers in Macedonia and Achaia" (v. 7). A transformation this complete, that happens this rapidly, is accomplished only when God is at work in people. They gave evidence of true salvation.

Examples for Believers (vv. 6–8)

The mimics became models. When the Thessalonians responded to the Gospel message, they "became imitators" of the missionaries and of the Lord (v. 6). They personalized in their own experience what they observed. Then, Paul says, they became models.

Example is a powerful means of communication, for good or bad. We imitate attitudes and actions. In Paul, Silas, and Timothy, the Thessalonians saw the example of three who were fully devoted followers of Christ. Right before them were examples for them to mimic. And as they imitated these three, they themselves became examples for others.

The power of example in modeling Christ flows through the first few verses of this chapter. These people were initially impressed with the Christlike examples of Paul, Silas, and Timothy. Consequently, Paul wrote, "You know how we lived among you for your sake" (v. 5). Furthermore, he continued, "You became imitators of us and of the Lord" (v. 6).

That sequence is important. These Christians first imitated the faith and lifestyle of these three missionaries, a pattern that then became the basis for imitating the Lord Jesus Christ.

The word translated "model" describes a stamp used to mint coins. The stamp literally left its mark on the metal. So these believers left their mark on others as their witness sounded forth throughout that region of the world, like stone-caused ripples on a pond.

▶ 16. The essence of disciple making is a discipler teaching and modeling for disciples. Each of us must be involved in disciple making. If you need to be discipled, whom can you ask to disciple you? Or perhaps you need to ask, "Who am I discipling and in what ways?" You must be a discipler if you are going to be obedient to Matthew 28:19–20 (in the margin).

Matthew 28:19–20

"'Therefore go and make disciples of all nations, baptizing them in the name of the Father and of the Son and of the Holy Spirit, and teaching them to obey everything I have commanded you. And surely I am with you always, to the very end of the age.'"

Expecting the Savior (v. 10)

Not only did they turn from idolatry to worship the true God, but they developed a sense of expectancy regarding the Second Coming of Jesus Christ. This is a vital Christian doctrine. Jesus Christ came into this world as the Son of God and died on the cross, but He also was buried and rose from the dead. He then ascended to heaven, promising that He would come again.

Even before His death, Jesus consoled His disciples with a message of hope—"I will come back!" (see John 14:1–3 in the margin). This promise was particularly meaningful to New Testament Christians who were undergoing intense persecution. They looked forward to deliverance. And this is why the doctrine of Christ's Second Coming was so encouraging to the Thessalonian believers.

There was no doubt about what turning to God meant to them. It meant complete forgiveness, the certainty of eternal life, and a returning Savior. It also gave them the strength they needed to endure the difficulties of the trials they faced. The word for "suffering" in verse 6 describes severe pressure. It is used in reference to pressing grapes in the process of making wine until they burst. It is not a word to describe mild discomfort but great difficulty. The difficulties this church faced could have included pressure from the Jews who stirred up a riot against Paul (Acts 17:5) and followed him to Berea (Acts 17:13). In addition, there was the opposition that came from within their own community (2:14).

To be like a model church requires two basic things. One is a model and the other is a willingness to change to be like that model. The change that is needed begins on the inside. If a congregation decides to implement the characteristics of the believers in Thessalonica, they will in time lapse back to what they were before. Characteristics come from character. If a church develops first the character, then the characteristics will come.

▶ 17. **If Paul sat down to write a letter to your church, how would he begin that letter? What would he thank God for? Would it be the activities in the church? Would he refer to the numerical growth? To the finely tuned organization? Or even to the size of the building? What would he say about the character of your church?**

_____
_____
_____
_____

John 14:1–3

"'Do not let your hearts be troubled. Trust in God; trust also in me. In my Father's house are many rooms; if it were not so, I would have told you. I am going there to prepare a place for you. And if I go and prepare a place for you, I will come back and take you to be with me that you also may be where I am.'"

Lesson 1: Character Counts

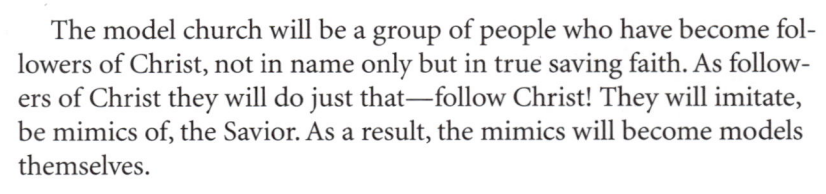

The model church will be a group of people who have become followers of Christ, not in name only but in true saving faith. As followers of Christ they will do just that—follow Christ! They will imitate, be mimics of, the Savior. As a result, the mimics will become models themselves.

The other character trait is vital as well, that of being people who are looking for the return of Jesus. That expectancy affects how we live. We need to live realizing that at any moment Jesus could call us home. That hope keeps us on our toes and encourages us, because the difficulties we may face today will not last forever.

Whether as an individual or as a church, to move forward in this backward world we must address first our character and then let it show in the characteristics of our life and of our church.

Small-Group Meeting 1

Opening Prayer

Begin with prayer. Ask God to bless your time of study together as you seek to understand the lessons from the Book of 1 Thessalonians and apply them to your life as well as your local church.

Building Relationships

Each of the "Building Relationships" suggestions ties in with this or the previous lesson. This activity helps the group get to know about the spiritual lives of the group members. Since the emphasis of Lesson 1 is on the people of a church, ask two or three members of your group to tell about when they became a Christian. After the testimonies, ask if anyone can share something specific in his life that changed after he was saved.

Reviewing the Lesson

1. Review the two major sections of this lesson—The Characteristics of a Model Church (p. 12) and The Character of a Model Church (p. 15). What were the three characteristics? What were the three aspects of character?

2. Point out the statement at the beginning of Part 3 (p. 15) that says, "Characteristics come from character." Ask how each of the characteristics comes from each of the aspects of character—for example, how is "work produced by faith" related to "evidence of salvation"? Help the group understand that our characteristics really do come from our character.

3. What are some things that you noticed in this lesson that were new to you?

Applying the Truths to Life

Select interactive questions to discuss as a group. Some are intended for personal reflection and are not for sharing with others. Be careful to choose ones that are for open discussion. Include some from each of the three parts of the lesson. Significant ones to include in this discussion are # 3 (p. 11), #10 (p. 13), and #12 (p. 14).

Ministering to One Another

One of the special blessings of being part of a small group is that you can be aware of each other's needs. Be sure to contact anyone who misses a meeting. Also, be prepared to help one another with personal needs, whether it is practical help, emotional support, or spiritual instruction.

Reaching Out to Others

You also need to decide if your group is an "open" or a "closed" group. Closed groups do not allow others to join after the first few times together. This allows for the group to develop more freedom in what is shared.

An open group intends for others to join. If yours is an open group, be sure all understand that. Take time in your first meeting to think of what you can do specifically to get others to come to your meetings. Every time your group meets, set an extra chair in the room as a reminder of getting someone to attend and sit in that seat.

Closing Prayer Time

Distribute sheets of paper that can be used to write down prayer requests. Encourage everyone to keep these with their study guides and bring them to every group meeting. Also, remember to use these during private prayer between group meetings. As the group grows more familiar with one another and develops greater trust that confidences will be kept, the requests will become more specific. Remind everyone of the importance of keeping confidences. These prayer times will help the group discover opportunities to minister to one another.

The leader should let everyone know who will close the prayer time.

LESSON 2

Building Blocks of Fruitful Ministry

1 Thessalonians 2:1–16

In Lewis Carroll's *Alice's Adventures in Wonderland*, Alice says to the Cheshire cat, "Would you tell me, please, which way I ought to go from here?" "That depends a good deal on where you want to get to," the cat replies. "I don't much care where," says Alice. "Then it doesn't matter which way you go," says the cat.

Many believers and churches operate on an "Alice in Wonderland" mentality, going somewhere and applying continued effort and concern to get there, but having no clear idea of where it is they wish to go. They do that in spite of the numerous times they have heard about the importance of goals, purpose, vision statements, having clear direction, and planning.

Then there are individuals and groups who have gone through a strategic planning process. Perhaps it was not terribly intentional but only a thinking through of what they wanted to be doing in four years. The first-year student, for example, begins his college career filling out a class schedule with a goal in mind—graduation. He has a basic plan in mind and selects his courses accordingly.

Strategic planning is not just for organizations. It can be for individuals as well. As Christians, we need to take time to think about how we want to live out our faith in a world that is heading the other direction.

An old cliché says that no one plans to fail but some fail to plan. That brings us back to the example of Alice. Do you know where you want to go? Do you care where you are going? It could be that you will live out the cliché not by planning to fail but by failing to plan.

▶ 1. What are some basic spiritual goals that you have? Think for a moment about some areas of your walk with the Lord that you want to develop, and then list a few goals. These might include reading the Bible daily or getting involved in a teaching ministry. Make your list now, and then later give more time to thinking through and praying about goals for your spiritual life.

_____

_____

_____

21

The world and the church are moving in opposite directions. That should be obvious. Also just as obvious is that God does not plan on the church failing. He said quite clearly that He would build His church and the gates of Hades would not overcome it (Matt. 16:18). It sounds like He has a plan! God's plan includes the church being fruitful, not a failure.

Paul's ministry in Thessalonica was not a failure but a fruitful one. While he does not give us specifics, he does give us the building blocks needed for a fruitful ministry. If our desire is to be fruitful, we will do well to learn from Paul these basic lessons for fruitful ministry.

PART 1: Interacting with the Scripture

Reading/Hearing God's Word

▶ 2. Using your Bible, read or listen to the passage of Scripture listed in the margin. As you begin, ask God to speak to you through His Word. Watch for verses or ideas that are especially meaningful to you today. Once you finish, check the box indicating that you have read the passage.

Meditating on God's Word

▶ 3. Write a brief summary of a meaningful verse or idea you noticed.

_____
_____
_____

Memorizing God's Word

▶ 4. During the time you are studying this lesson, commit to memory 1 Thessalonians 2:13 (in the margin). Memorizing this key verse will help you remember the important points of this lesson.

Understanding God's Word

▶ 5. Read again the focal passage for this week's lesson (1 Thess. 2:3–4, 7–8, 11) in the margin. Underline any key phrases or ideas that seem especially meaningful to you.

Read or Listen to:

☐ 1 Thessalonians 2:1–16

1 Thessalonians 2:13

"And we also thank God continually because, when you received the word of God, which you heard from us, you accepted it not as the word of men, but as it actually is, the word of God."

1 Thessalonians 2:3–4, 7–8, 11

"For the appeal we make does not spring from error or impure motives, nor are we trying to trick you. On the contrary, we speak as men approved by God to be entrusted with the gospel. We are not trying to please men by God, who tests our hearts.

". . . but we were gentle among you, like a mother caring for her little children. We loved you so much that we were delighted to share with you not only the gospel of God but our lives as well, because you had become so dear to us. . . .

"For you know that we dealt with each of you as a father deals with his own children."

LESSON 2: BUILDING BLOCKS OF FRUITFUL MINISTRY   23

▶ 6. Look back at these verses. Circle one of the underlined phrases or words that you would like to understand or experience more fully.

Looking through the Scripture to God

Now pause to pray. "Lord, help me to see the need to think through what I am doing to be fruitful for You in this world. Also help me to be a faithful part of the church, so that together with my brothers and sisters in Christ we can build fruitful ministries."

PART 2: A Fruitful Ministry Must Be Faithful (2:1–6)

The first building block Paul gives us is that of faithfulness. As you read the beginning of 1 Thessalonians 2, various aspects of faithfulness are evident. In this section the faithfulness described is not the "stick-to-itive" kind of faithfulness, but a fidelity to God's Word that affects both the message and the messenger.

Biblical in Content (vv. 2–4, 8–9, 13)

Paul made it clear that the authority for what he, Silas, and Timothy were teaching was from God (v. 4). The Lord Himself was the divine Source of their message. Though all of the apostles were given special authority by Jesus Christ to preach the Gospel, Paul in a special way received that message directly from God (see Galatians 1:12 in the margin). His intent was to be faithful to that message, keeping both his message and his ministry biblical in content.

▶ 7. Do you consistently read the Bible? What is your plan for reading? You cannot "know" the Word if you do not read it. Ask someone in your small group to share his or her plan. If it is working for others, it may work for you.

▶ 8. What do you believe? Rate on a scale of 1 to 10 how much you believe the following:

 ___ what you read in the newspaper

 ___ e-mails forwarded to you that say, "This really is true!"

 ___ information shared in the office break room

 ___ the Bible

 ___ talk show "guests"

 ___ political campaign advertisements

Galatians 1:12

"I did not receive it [the gospel I preached] from any man, nor was I taught it; rather, I received it by revelation from Jesus Christ."

Paul, Silas, and Timothy did not come to Thessalonica to say things that would ingratiate themselves with people. They were not politicians seeking votes. They didn't soften their message to win a hearing and to please the crowd. They simply preached the Gospel of Jesus Christ—that we are all sinners and need a Savior. They did not give their opinions; they proclaimed the Word. Their message was not false, their motive was not impure, and their method was not misleading. The word Paul used that is translated "trick" in verse 3 ("nor are we trying to trick you") signifies "catching fish with bait"—in other words, trapping the Thessalonians in some kind of religious system.

Evangelistic tactics of some religious cults are designed with deceit in mind. Their initial presentations sound very biblical and harmless. But when a person becomes entangled in their religious system, he is then taught false doctrine. At that point it is very difficult to discern truth from error. In contrast, what Paul and the others said and did were from hearts that desired to please God. You cannot please God with deceitful ministries.

▶ **9. What are some examples of false claims that religious groups make?**

_____

_____

_____

▶ **10. Do you always tell the truth? Remember, it is easy to twist the truth—even when we don't intend to.**

These are bold statements from Paul, ones that claim purity of heart. He said this because he knew that God tests our hearts (v. 4). A tested heart is one that has been sifted and found fit. Paul and the other missionaries had tested hearts and trusted hands. They were tested by God and trusted.

We should desire to be biblical in this same way—and we should desire our churches to be so as well. In a world that thinks truth is not absolute but is relative, we go against the prevailing winds when we remain biblical in content and become known as a place that tells the truth, with conviction based on the bedrock of God's Word and not on the shifting sands of human opinion.

Authentic in Nature (vv. 5–6)

In these verses the emphasis shifts from the message to the messenger. While others may have used deceitful methods and motives to sway the Thessalonians, Paul and the others did not. They did not engage in smooth talking in an attempt to make a favorable impression to gain influence. The Greek word translated as "flattery" (v. 5) presents a concept difficult to explain. Flattery, as we use the word in the English language, is not exactly what Paul had in mind. Some scholars suggest that "cajolery" is more the sense of the word. This is the use of acceptable speech with the purpose of lulling another into a false sense of security so that one may obtain one's own ends.

Paul also points out that he, Timothy, and Silas did not pretend to be poor as a pretense to get rich in ministry or seek personal glory. Evidently, all three of these missionaries had been accused of having selfish reasons for being in Thessalonica—to see what they could get out of these people for personal gain. No doubt this criticism came from false teachers who knew their own hearts very well. It was not uncommon for religious leaders to take advantage of people financially. There were many people in the religious world of Paul's day with one primary motive—material gain. Consequently, as the letter to the Thessalonians reveals, Paul sometimes bent over backwards to make sure people could not accuse him of greed.

Nor were Paul and the others looking for the praise of men (v. 6). They were in Thessalonica to glorify God, not themselves. Had they been seeking self-glorification, certainly there would have been better ways to obtain it. Why subject yourself to persecution, even endangering your life? To accuse Paul and his fellow missionaries of this kind of motivation is to completely ignore the facts.

1 Corinthians 2:1–5

"When I came to you, brothers, I did not come with eloquence or superior wisdom as I proclaimed to you the testimony about God. For I resolved to know nothing while I was with you except Jesus Christ and him crucified. I came to you in weakness and fear, and with much trembling. My message and my preaching were not with wise and persuasive words, but with a demonstration of the Spirit's power, so that your faith might not rest on men's wisdom, but on God's power."

▶ **11. Do you use any form of deception to achieve a goal? This is related to telling the truth, but it goes further. It involves our methodology—using ways and means to trick people into making decisions that ultimately will lead them down a path they otherwise might not take. Are you careful to be authentic at church?**

The method they used was authenticity. This was Paul's pattern, particularly as seen in his ministry among the Corinthians (see 1 Corinthians 2:1–5 in the margin). Once you eliminate such things as flattery, pretense, and seeking praise as possible motivations for their ministry, about all that's left is being real. It has been said that you are real when you say real things about real issues with real feelings. This is true only if you are real, living what you are, telling the truth, and admitting your failures and weakness. Be real, and your ministry will be real.

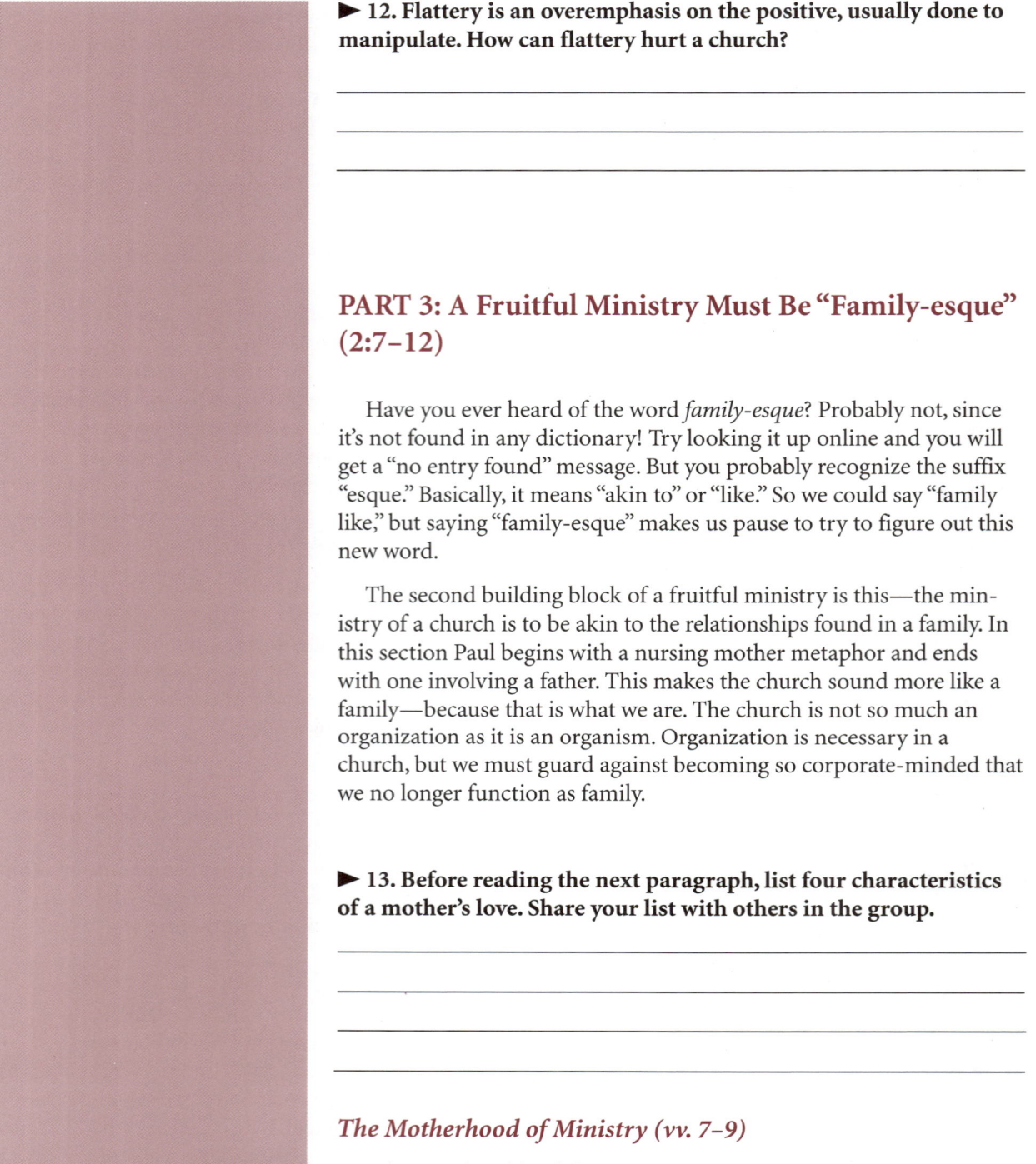

▶ **12. Flattery is an overemphasis on the positive, usually done to manipulate. How can flattery hurt a church?**

_____

_____

_____

PART 3: A Fruitful Ministry Must Be "Family-esque" (2:7–12)

Have you ever heard of the word *family-esque*? Probably not, since it's not found in any dictionary! Try looking it up online and you will get a "no entry found" message. But you probably recognize the suffix "esque." Basically, it means "akin to" or "like." So we could say "family like," but saying "family-esque" makes us pause to try to figure out this new word.

The second building block of a fruitful ministry is this—the ministry of a church is to be akin to the relationships found in a family. In this section Paul begins with a nursing mother metaphor and ends with one involving a father. This makes the church sound more like a family—because that is what we are. The church is not so much an organization as it is an organism. Organization is necessary in a church, but we must guard against becoming so corporate-minded that we no longer function as family.

▶ **13. Before reading the next paragraph, list four characteristics of a mother's love. Share your list with others in the group.**

_____

_____

_____

_____

The Motherhood of Ministry (vv. 7–9)

When Paul and his fellow missionaries left the church at Thessalonica, they were deeply concerned about the spiritual welfare of these new Christians (vv. 7–9). Consequently, they sent Timothy back to see how the Thessalonians were doing in living out their faith (3:1–5). Timothy's report was encouraging, even though false teachers had tried to discredit their ministry there. Paul wrote to the church, presenting a subtle defense against these criticisms, and then moved into a very positive stance regarding the kind of ministry they had with

Lesson 2: Building Blocks of Fruitful Ministry

these people. To illustrate their mutual ministry among them, Paul referred first of all to the relationship that should exist between a loving mother and her newborn child. That involves the following:

• Gentle care (v. 7). With gentleness, sensitivity, and kindness toward people, Paul and the others carried out ministry in Thessalonica. These men loved the Thessalonians from and with their hearts and souls—with their total beings, as a mother loves her child.

• Loving sharing (v. 8). There is no more intimate and beautiful picture of unconditional love than that of a mother caring for her newborn and giving herself totally to this child. In such a manner, Paul stated, they treated the newborn Christians in Thessalonica.

• Diligent laboring (v. 9). A mother's work is never done, and sometimes it seems as if she is always doing it. As Paul compared ministry with motherhood, he mentioned how diligently they worked in ministry for the believers there.

▶ 14. Give an example of how each of these characteristics Paul listed—gentle care, loving sharing, and diligent laboring—can be practiced in your church.

_____

_____

_____

For our ministries to be fruitful we need these three elements in abundance.

▶ 15. Before reading the next paragraph, list four things that are characteristic of a father's love. Share your list with others in the group.

_____

_____

_____

_____

The Fatherhood of Ministry (vv. 10–12)

As Paul reflected on the spiritual growth of these new Christians, he expanded his parental illustration of the relationship they enjoyed with the Thessalonians. While some ministry is compared to the work of a mother, other ministry is more like a father's role. Notice the specific ways this "paternal" care is illustrated.

• An exemplary model (v. 10). Paul first reminded these believers of the way in which they had demonstrated Christ among them: "You are witnesses, and so is God," he wrote, "of how holy, righteous and blameless we were among you who believed." Paul, Silas, and Timothy not only told these Christians how to live, but they also showed them how to live. They were a living demonstration of Christ's holy and righteous life.

• A personal ministry (v. 11). The father-child analogy Paul uses here has two important dimensions. The first, as we've just seen, is that modeling Christ is foundational. The second is the necessity of dealing with each person as an individual. No child in any family is identical to the others in terms of personal needs. We must not treat all children alike. This, Paul implies, is part of a father's parenting responsibility.

As parents deal individually with their own children, so we must personalize our ministry to others. That's why Paul wrote to these believers, "We dealt with each of you as a father deals with his own children."

How this happened we do not know. Perhaps these three men divided up the church among themselves and made sure that each person was ministered to by one of them. Perhaps they selected other mature and growing Christians in the group to help them carry out this process. But whatever the method, it is clear that their ministry was individualized. They encouraged each one, comforted each one, and urged each one "to live lives worthy of God" (v. 12).

▶ **16. The primary characteristics Paul lists of fatherhood are modeling and dealing with each person as an individual. Give an example of how each of these can be practiced in your church.**

_____
_____
_____

This is ministry by family, not force. Paul and the others demonstrated gentleness and love while dealing with these believers in a way that imparted not only truth but their own lives as well. A fruitful ministry cannot just be organized—it must be incarnated, made flesh by real people living out real relationships in the family of God.

PART 4: A Fruitful Ministry Must Have Fortitude (2:13–16)

A subtle change now takes place, one that could easily go unnoticed. Paul switches his emphasis from himself and Timothy and Silas to the Thessalonians. Now he is encouraging them in their witness, because if ministry is to be fruitful, it must have fortitude, especially in the face of opposition. He gives very specific statements in these verses that encourage us to have fortitude in our ministries.

Remember that the Bible is the Word of God (v. 13)

One of the greatest encouragements for fortitude when we are experiencing difficulty in ministry is remembering that the word we preach and teach is the Word of God. You are not dealing with the word of men or some teaching that is tailored to fit the popular knowledge of the day. The Word is God-centered, not man-centered. It is not changeable, nor does it mirror current thought. The Bible is the Word of God, which works in our lives.

Recognize that you are not the only one opposed (vv. 14–15)

Persecution for their new faith was not a surprise to the Thessalonians, nor should it be a surprise to us. Paul had warned them it would come (3:4). When facing opposition, we should imitate other witnesses. In this sense the Thessalonians "became imitators of God's churches in Judea" (v. 14). Paul was referring to the fact that many Jews in Judea had turned to Christ, and as a result they were persecuted by their fellow Jews. Paul, of course, knew all about this firsthand because he was the chief persecutor before he became a Christian (see Acts 8:3 in the margin).

Paul seemed to be saying that the Jews who lived in Thessalonica did the same thing to the church there that other Jews did to the churches in Judea. Luke records that many unbelieving Jews in Thessalonica "were jealous." They were the ones who "rounded up some bad characters from the marketplace, formed a mob and started a riot in the city" (Acts 17:5). It was the Jews of Thessalonica who initiated the persecution and eventually drove these missionaries out of town.

Wherever you are there will be opposition. The church is moving forward according to God's purpose and plan. The world is not. We live not in an "anti-religious" age but in an "anti-Christ" one. The opposition is not to religion or spirituality but to the specific claims of Christ. And make no mistake: it is opposition, not just indifference. Those who oppose the truth of the Gospel are in essence hostile to all men, for keeping God's message from men is an act of hostility toward all men. Clearly, as Paul teaches in these verses, the need for fortitude today is real.

Acts 8:3

"Saul began to destroy the church. Going from house to house, he dragged off men and women and put them in prison."

Realize that the issue is salvation (v. 16)

A statement in the *Disciple's Study Bible* says, "Stopping the mission of God's church is sin."[1] The seriousness of hindering the preaching of the Gospel message is seen in this verse. Those who do so "heap up their sins to the limit." Paul knew that those who opposed the Gospel would one day face the wrath of God.

This realization should eliminate any hesitancy to share our faith. The importance of our individual involvement in outreach is a biblical truth that we must not only believe but also incorporate into our lives. As we study God's Word, we come to realize that people matter dearly to God, that people are lost and must be reached with the Gospel, and that people need to be reached by *us*. We need to be ready and willing to reach out—and then do it. True, our culture will not always accept or appreciate our evangelistic efforts. We will be opposed—which brings us back to this essential building block of a fruitful ministry. We need fortitude.

▶ **17. What are some of the specific ways you think your church is facing opposition to its ministry? Take time right now to pray that God will give your congregation fortitude.**

▶ **18. Make a prayer list for yourself and for others in your group. Put on that list some of the special challenges you and they are facing. Commit to praying regularly for fortitude.**

All Christians face a variety of tasks and challenges. And there are thousands of university programs designed to equip us to perform these tasks and meet these challenges. But there is no course more important to prepare us to face life—in any situation—than the Word of God. It is foundational to all we do. The fruitful ministry must be faithful to it.

All churches face a variety of ministry opportunities that need a special touch or a direct intervention. Paul calls our attention to a model that must be at the heart of our ministries. It is not that of a corporation but of a family, one in which there is a loving mother and an instructing father. The fruitful ministry must be family-esque.

All Christians must expect opposition. A fact of the spiritual war raging in the unseen realms is that as we seek to serve God, we will be opposed. Our world accepts and adores those who oppose the ones faithfully ministering the Word of God. That is why we must have fortitude in our ministries if we are to be fruitful.

Small-Group Meeting 2

Opening Prayer

Begin with prayer. Ask God to help you be open to learning new ideas from this lesson on the building blocks for a fruitful ministry, to be challenged to advance the ministry of your local church.

Building Relationships

Ask two or three people to tell about times that they really felt the blessing of being a part of the family of God. It will probably be easier to think of examples of "the motherhood of ministry," but perhaps someone will share about experiencing "the fatherhood of ministry."

Reviewing the Lesson

1. Review the three basic building blocks for a fruitful ministry, taking time to define each of the three significant words: faithful, family-esque, and fortitude.

2. In what ways did the Christians in Thessalonica demonstrate their faithfulness?

3. List the basic elements of the "motherhood" and "fatherhood" of ministry (pp. 26-27).

4. Read again 1 Thessalonians 1:13–16. Note the specific difficulties Paul faced. What are some of the difficulties that Christians face in ministry today?

Applying the Truths to Life

Select interactive questions to discuss as a group. Some are intended for personal reflection and are not for sharing with others. Be careful to choose ones that are for open discussion. Include some from each of the four parts of the lesson. Significant ones to include in this discussion are #9 (p. 24), #12 (p. 26), #17 (p. 30), and #18 (p. 30).

Ministering to One Another

Does someone in the group need to rely not only on God but also on you? Read Galatians 6:2 aloud. Perhaps God at this time wants your small group to help bear the burden of another. Ask God to make you aware of such an opportunity. It might be someone in your group or someone whom your group knows.

Reaching Out to Others

If yours is an open group, did you set an empty chair in your circle? What will you do to fill it next time you meet?

Closing Prayer Time

Ask everyone to get out his or her prayer sheets. Go through them item by item and ask for an update. The group leader can start keeping a special page of answered prayers. When the study group finishes this guide, it will be a special blessing to look over the list of prayer requests that became praises because you prayed. As the group grows more familiar with one another and develops greater trust that confidences will be kept, the requests will become more specific. Remind everyone of the importance of keeping confidences. These prayer times will help the group discover opportunities to minister to one another.

Close the time together with group prayer. Use this time to pray specifically that God would impress upon each heart the desire to see these building blocks for ministry be characteristics of your local church. Also, ask God to help you participate in building up the body of believers in Christlikeness.

The leader should let everyone know who will close the prayer time.

LESSON 3

"*I* Get Down"

1 Thessalonians 2:17–3:13

So send I you to labor unrewarded,
To serve unpaid, unloved, unsought, unknown,
To bear rebuke, to suffer scorn and scoffing—
So send I you to toil for Me alone.

The hymn "So Send I You" has been considered by many to be the finest missionary hymn of the 20th century, used in countless missionary conferences and church services as a song to challenge people to full-time vocational ministry in missions. Read the above verse again, this time not allowing familiarity to keep you from hearing what it says. It is a one-sided song, telling only the sorrows and privations of the missionary call and none of its triumphs.

The poem that was set to music by John W. Peterson was written by E. Margaret Clarkson, a 23-year-old schoolteacher in a gold-mining camp town in northern Ontario, Canada, at a time in which she experienced loneliness of every kind—mental, cultural, and particularly spiritual. During a seven-year period of teaching in the remote regions of Canada, she never found real Christian fellowship. Churches were modern and born-again Christians almost non-existent. One night while meditating on the loneliness of her situation she wrote those words, which arrest our attention to the fact that sometimes we get down—even when we are serving Jesus.

▶ **1. This study begins at a low point, but keep reading. It will get better. Still, we need to realize that sometimes we struggle emotionally. Is there a particular time you can remember when you "got down"?**

_____
_____
_____

33

In this section of Paul's letter, he opened his heart and revealed his humanness, his emotions. It is true that Paul used the plural pronouns *we* and *our* and *us* throughout this section, but the focus is clearly on his personal feelings and emotional reactions, both in a positive and negative sense.

Here we see Paul, the man, the human being. This is encouraging since we tend to idealize people of his stature, falsely concluding that they somehow lived above the emotional struggles and difficulties of life. Not so! And Paul's personal openness at this point in his letter demonstrates his internal struggles. More important than his emotions, however, are the actions he took when he experienced these emotions.

▶ **2. If someone who was down asked you to help him get back up, what are some things that you might do or advise him to do?**

_____

_____

_____

PART 1: Interacting with the Scripture

Reading/Hearing God's Word

▶ **3. Using your Bible, read or listen to the passage of Scripture listed in the margin. As you begin, ask God to speak to you through His Word. Watch for verses or ideas that are especially meaningful to you today. Once you finish, check the box indicating that you have read the passage.**

Meditating on God's Word

▶ **4. Write a brief summary of a meaningful verse or idea you noticed.**

_____

_____

_____

Memorizing God's Word

▶ **5. During the time you are studying this lesson, commit to memory 1 Thessalonians 3:12–13 (in the margin). Memorizing these key verses will help you remember the important points of this lesson.**

Read or Listen to:

☐ 1 Thessalonians 2:17–3:13

1 Thessalonians 3:12–13

"May the Lord make your love increase and overflow for each other and for everyone else, just as ours does for you. May he strengthen your hearts so that you will be blameless and holy in the presence of our God and Father when our Lord Jesus comes with all his glory."

LESSON 3: "I GET DOWN"

> **1 Thessalonians 2:17–20**
>
> "But, brothers, when we were torn away from you for a short time (in person, not in thought), out of our intense longing we made every effort to see you. For we wanted to come to you—certainly I, Paul, did, again and again—but Satan stopped us. For what is our hope, our joy, or the crown in which we will glory in the presence of our Lord Jesus when he comes? Is it not you? Indeed, you are our glory and joy."

Understanding God's Word

▶ 6. Read again the focal passage for this week's lesson (1 Thess. 2:17–20) in the margin. Underline any key phrases or ideas that seem especially meaningful to you.

▶ 7. Look back at these verses. Circle one of the underlined phrases or words that you would like to understand or experience more fully.

Looking through the Scripture to God

 Now pause to pray. "I am human, Father, and sometimes struggle emotionally. Thank You for giving me insight into the emotions of Paul as he served You. May I learn how to have a heart strengthened to serve."

PART 2: At Times Our Heart Will Ache (2:17–20)

To understand more fully what Paul was feeling, we need to look more carefully at the reasons for his anxiety.

Hurt by the Separation (v. 17)

This reference takes us back to those difficult days described in Acts 17 when the Jews became jealous and "formed a mob and started a riot in the city" (Acts 17:5). The persecution became so intense that Paul and Silas had to flee for their lives.

Again, we see a correlation with the father and mother illustrations Paul used earlier in the letter. These people were his "children" in Christ. He had cared for them like a nursing mother and had encouraged and comforted them like a caring and nurturing father (2:7, 11). Now he uses another family term of endearment by addressing them as brothers. The word translated "torn away," *aporphanisthentes*, means, "when we were orphaned." Paul's family instincts were dealt a blow by the forced separation, but to be out of sight was not to be out of mind. Still, the pain Paul felt is evident in this verse because these people mattered dearly to him.

▶ **8. Paul was really connected to these people, so much so that he felt orphaned when he left. How connected do you feel to the people of your church? What are some specific things that can be done to help develop and strengthen the family cohesiveness of a congregation?**

_____

_____

_____

Hindered by Satan (v. 18)

Paul's ache was caused by more than the environmental barriers that kept him from going back to Thessalonica. He was also in a battle with Satan himself. Thus he wrote, "For we wanted to come to you—certainly I, Paul, did, again and again—but Satan stopped us" (v. 18).

Notice that Paul had endeavored to return to Thessalonica on several occasions. But each time he was blocked by the greatest evil personality in the universe—the devil himself. Spiritual battle may be an unseen conflict, but it is real. Daniel knew the reality of this opposition as the answer to his praying was delayed by the warfare in heaven (Dan. 10:12–13). Likewise, the account of the birth of Christ in Revelation 12:4–5 gives us a glimpse into the reality of Satan's opposition.

Paul does not tell us specifically how he was prevented from returning to Thessalonica. The word translated as "stopped" in verse 18 describes the breaking up of a road and putting up obstacles, a tactic of war. Certainly, Satan works in a multitude of different ways to thwart God's work. However, here it appears that Satan was in some way directly involved in these circumstances. He truly deserves to be called "Adversary" (see 1 Peter 5:8 in the margin).

It is possible that Paul was referring to the way Satan used those who opposed the apostle's ministry. If this is true, we can more clearly understand the dynamics involved. Certainly, there is no question that the Jews, who openly and violently opposed Jesus Christ, were controlled by Satan. This is why Jesus so bluntly stated, "You belong to your father, the devil, and you want to carry out your father's desires" (John 8:44).

Why would Satan do this? Because he knew that Paul's heart was for the good of the people, and what was good for the people was the ministry of God's Word to them. These people also mattered dearly to God.

1 Peter 5:8

"Be sober, be vigilant; because your adversary the devil, as a roaring lion, walketh about, seeking whom he may devour (KJV)."

► 9. Satan still works against God's people. What are some of the tactics he uses today?
___
___
___

Heart Stayed Sincere (v. 19)

Paul's actions in response to what he was feeling are more important than the emotions themselves. But before learning of his responses to these difficulties we are given this insight into the heart of Paul: it stayed sincere, in spite of all the troubles he was experiencing. The people to whom and for whom he ministered kept Paul moving forward. They were his hope, joy, and crown! He looked forward to the day when in the presence of Jesus he could present them as people who had been won for the Gospel. His focus was not on just the immediate situation but on eternity, and not on earthly rewards but eternal ones, a wreath of exaltation that would be his in that day.

► 10. Even the joy of being with family and friends can be lessened if we think about the long drive to their house. Read Revelation 22:1–5. What aspects about heaven mentioned in this passage encourage you today?
___
___
___

PART 3: At Times We Will Feel Pain in Our Work (3:1–5)

Paul was vitally concerned about the believers at Thessalonica. While undoubtedly he had concerns about their physical well-being, his main concern at this point was their spiritual well-being. He knew what he had gone through in the way of Satanic opposition to his ministry, and he feared that they might have likewise suffered spiritual damage.

► 11. Consider your daily prayer list. You probably pray for the physical needs of your family, friends, and of those in your church. But are you praying for the spiritual needs of others too? What are

---

Revelation 22:1–5

"Then the angel showed me the river of the water of life, as clear as crystal, flowing from the throne of God and of the Lamb down the middle of the great street of the city. On each side of the river stood the tree of life, bearing twelve crops of fruit, yielding its fruit every month. And the leaves of the tree are for the healing of the nations. No longer will there be any curse. The throne of God and of the Lamb will be in the city, and his servants will serve him. They will see his face, and his name will be on their foreheads. There will be no more night. They will not need the light of a lamp or the light of the sun, for the Lord God will give them light. And they will reign for ever and ever."

some specific examples of spiritual needs that people might have—and for which you should pray?

_____

_____

_____

The Suspense (v. 1)

There came a point where they could "stand it no longer" (v. 1). Paul was afraid Satan might have led these new believers astray. This concern is one of the primary reasons Paul was so eager to return to Thessalonica. "I was afraid," he wrote, "that in some way the tempter might have tempted you and our efforts might have been useless" (v. 3). His anxiety became so intense that he had no choice but to do something about it. This is a highly emotional statement—Paul's anxiety and deep concern for these people were becoming intolerable.

The Sending (vv. 2–4)

Paul evidently felt very good about the Thessalonians' initial response to his ministry. But it wasn't until he received a positive report from Timothy that he was absolutely sure that these people were truly converted to Jesus Christ. How had they stood up to the persecution once he and his fellow missionaries had left? Had the Word of God really taken root in their lives? Were they truly born again? Were they growing in faith and hope and love?

Paul's anxiety over these unanswered questions motivated him to action. He decided to stay in Athens and to send Timothy back to Thessalonica. This was a very difficult decision. He wanted to go personally, but probably knew that his presence in Thessalonica might accentuate the persecution against the believers there—giving Satan the opportunity he needed to accomplish his insidious goals. Since Timothy's profile was much lower than his, he decided to send his missionary companion.

▶ 12. Sometimes we need a friend or need to be a friend. Our physical presence can mean so much. How can each of the following be used to answer our prayers for the spiritual needs of someone?

• a phone call

_____

• a note in the mail

_____

- **an e-mail**

- **a shared lunch time**

- **going to his or her home**

- **"mall walking" together**

- **sharing a pew at church**

He sent Timothy to find out about the solidity of the Thessalonians' faith (v. 3). Though this reason for Timothy's trip appears second in this section of the letter, it is the primary reason he returned according to verse 5. Paul wanted to know if their faith was real.

The other reason for Timothy's visit is found in verse 2. Timothy brought to the church what we could refer to as "spiritual steroids." While steroids have been abused in our day, particularly by those wanting to enhance their athletic performance, when properly used under medical supervision they do build up and strengthen. The Greek word here is *sterizai*. It means to "make firm and solid" and is the origin of the English word *steroid*. It was Paul's intent for Timothy to strengthen, encourage, and settle them in their faith. There was nothing at all negative about these "spiritual steroids"!

▶ **13. What verse can you give to someone else that might be a "spiritual steroid" for him or her?**

He encouraged them (v. 2) by coming alongside to speak to them words of encouragement, a different word than the one translated "strengthen." This encouragement came from Paul and ultimately from God. Again, the Greek word translated "encourage" is picturesque, as it literally means "by the side, to call" and speaks of calling someone to come alongside and help. Paul did not want them to be unsettled by the trials. He knew what it was like to experience such difficulties and had warned of their coming (v. 4). His concern was that they not be shaken by them.

Much of the persecution Paul faced involved his physical well-being, which he described graphically when he wrote to the Corinthians (see 2 Corinthians 11:24–27 in the margin). He culminates that very graphic paragraph by referring to that which was creating his greatest anxiety regarding the Thessalonians. "Besides everything else," he concluded, "I face daily the pressure of my concern for all the churches" (2 Cor. 11:28).

Sidetracked (v. 5)

Though Paul was concerned whether these people had become true believers, he felt that evidence indicated they were members of the family of God. But Paul also knew what persecution could do to new Christians. He knew that they could be sidetracked from the will of God and waver in their faith. In his anxiety, Paul also expressed feelings of fear. Though the word *fear* is not used in the original language of the New Testament, it is certainly implied in Paul's statement. Furthermore, anyone who can identify with Paul's concern about these people can also identify with his emotions. Fear is a more specific manifestation of anxiety and can be very intense and difficult to handle. For most people, it's the kind of emotion that can lead to sleepless nights. Thus, Paul sent Timothy.

▶ 14. Complete the following: "I can be spiritually sidetracked by . . ." Possible answers include sports, shopping, movies, and work. Make your list; perhaps write it in red with the words "Dangerous Intersections" across the top.

_____

_____

_____

It may sound simplistic to say, "Satan was at work." But with that simplicity there is the somber reminder that Satan's efforts are directed to hinder or even destroy our faith. Paul's attachment to the people of the church in Thessalonica caused an ache in his heart and pain in his work, especially due to the suspense. It might seem like enough to discourage anyone from involvement in ministry, but there is more—and it is encouraging.

---

2 Corinthians 11:24–27

"Five times I received from the Jews the forty lashes minus one. Three times I was beaten with rods, once I was stoned, three times I was shipwrecked, I spent a night and a day in the open sea, I have been constantly on the move. I have been in danger from rivers, in danger from bandits, in danger from my own countrymen, in danger from Gentiles; in danger in the city, in danger in the country, in danger at sea; and in danger from false brothers. I have labored and toiled and have often gone without sleep; I have known hunger and thirst and have often gone without food; I have been cold and naked."

PART 4: At Times We Need Aspirin for Our Souls (3:6–13)

The church in Thessalonica seemed to have everything. It is described as a model church with a model type of ministry, but now this section of 1 Thessalonians switches to a description of the emotions of ministry. It includes the positive report from Timothy, which was like aspirin to an aching soul.

Timothy brought "good news" (v. 6). Usually Paul reserved that phrase to describe the Gospel, but here he mentions three things that caused him joy—their faith, love, and attitude toward him. Paul was encouraged by the report on their faith and their firm stand.

Paul used the word *encouraged* to describe his emotional reaction to Timothy's positive report. This, of course, is predictable, and all of us can identify with the good feelings that are associated with this word. It was exciting to him to know that things were going well with those whom he loved. "Now we really live," Paul wrote, "since you are standing firm in the Lord" (v. 8).

This statement has strong emotional overtones. Paul was not saying that they were literally "staying alive" because of Timothy's report. Rather, he was saying, "We are so excited about what is happening to you that we have courage to go on teaching and preaching the Gospel with a new fervor and excitement." The positive report regarding the Thessalonians gave him a new surge of energy, a new zest for living the Christian life, and a new motivation to carry on the ministry that God had called him to.

All of this brought joy to Paul. Joy, of course, is one of the most positive emotions a human being experiences. Paul experienced it because of the Thessalonians. His anxiety was dissipated with a feeling of happiness. And so he wrote, "How can we thank God enough for you in return for all the joy we have in the presence of our God because of you?" (v. 9).

▶ **15. What is the difference between "joy" and "happiness"? A hint here—notice how similar the word *happiness* is to *happenings*.**

_____

_____

_____

Paul's perspective on joy was both present and future. Earlier he had written, "For what is our hope, our joy, or the crown in which we will glory in the presence of our Lord Jesus when he comes? Is it not you?

Indeed, you are our glory and joy" (2:19–20). Paul was referring to that day when they would together stand in the presence of Jesus Christ and rejoice together. The greatest joy for Paul would be to see these believers in heaven.

But Paul's joy was also a part of his earthly experience. And in this instance it was directly related to the way in which these believers had stood firm in their faith, in spite of persecution. Again, to understand more fully what Paul was actually feeling, we need to look more specifically at the reasons for his positive emotions.

Timothy had brought good news about the Thessalonian believers' faith and love (v. 6). That report is why Paul began this letter by thanking God for their "work produced by faith" and their "labor prompted by love" (1:3). Timothy had just reported on the state of the Thessalonian church—and Paul was elated.

Timothy also had reported that the Thessalonian Christians had "pleasant memories" and longed "to see" them again (v. 6). From a human point of view, this part of the report probably lifted Paul's spirits more than anything. Paul and his fellow missionaries had demonstrated their love for these people in unusual ways. They had "worked night and day in order not to be a burden to anyone" (2:9). Like a nursing mother they had tenderly cared for them (2:7). Like a loving father they had nurtured them one by one (2:11–12). They had literally risked their lives so that they might share the Gospel with these people (2:2).

To receive a report that these Christians had forgotten what Paul and his fellow missionaries had done or, worse yet, to hear that they had unpleasant memories would have devastated these men emotionally. So we can understand Paul's positive response. These people remembered and longed to see them again just as Paul, Silas, and Timothy longed to see them.

Timothy reported that these Christians were "standing firm in the Lord" (3:8). This relates directly to their "endurance inspired by hope" (1:3). No one or no thing—false teachers, persecution, or Satan himself—had diverted them from their hope in Jesus Christ. From a divine perspective, this was the greatest news Timothy reported. Paul's concern that they may have become "unsettled by these trials" (3:3) had been one of the major causes for his anxiety.

▶ **16. Are negative emotions normal?** ☐ Yes or ☐ No

▶ **17. Are negative emotions permanent—once here they can never go away?** ☐ Yes or ☐ No

When Paul experienced negative emotions, he took action. He sought solutions for the concerns that were creating so much anxiety. And when he experienced positive emotions that resulted from his earlier actions in sending Timothy to check on the Thessalonians' spiritual welfare, he also responded with specific action steps.

Paul thanked God for this good report (v. 9). He knew that all glory must go to God even for those things that involve our personal efforts. Ultimately, God must be glorified in all we do.

Paul continued to pray that he might see them again and help them even more (vv. 10–11). You might think that Paul would have been satisfied with Timothy's report and desired to go on to greener pastures. Not so! He still wanted to see the Thessalonian Christians and encourage them even more. What a tremendous example of a man with a shepherd's heart!

Paul prayed for the Thessalonians' continued spiritual growth in love and holiness (vv. 12–13). His prayer speaks for itself. He desired that they would have an increasing, overflowing love for each other and for everyone else. Also, he wished for their hearts to be strengthened so that they would be blameless in holiness, free from any reasonable charge by others, and set apart for God, in their hearts and in their habits. He truly had found aspirin for his soul.

This section of 1 Thessalonians takes us through a variety of emotions. Paul described the aches and pains of ministry as well as the aspirin. The reality of ministry is that there will be times we get down—but we do not have to stay down.

▶ **18. Review the three actions Paul took when he was "down." Pray right now, asking God to help you remember that there are things you must do when you are down.**

Several years after writing "So Send I You," Margaret Clarkson became dissatisfied with what she had written. She began to realize that it was very one-sided; it told only the sorrows and privations of the missionary call and none of its triumphs. So she wrote another poem in the same rhythm so that verses could be used interchangeably, this time focusing on the glory and the hope of the missionary calling.

So send I you, by grace made strong to triumph

O'er hosts of hell, o'er darkness, death and sin,

My name to bear, and in that name to conquer.

So send I you, My victory to win.

Small-Group Meeting 3

Opening Prayer

Begin this meeting with a time of silent prayer. Allow everyone to go "one on one" with God for a moment, asking Him to help them in the times of discouragement to determine to continue doing what He wants, by grace being made strong to triumph. The group leader can bring this time of silent prayer to a conclusion by praying aloud.

Building Relationships

We all have times when we are discouraged or hurt. Ask if someone has a story to share about a time when he or she was particularly struggling with discouragement and what brought encouragement during that experience.

Reviewing the Lesson

1. Remind the group of the focus of the lesson: the reality of ministry is that there will be times we get down, but we do not have to stay down. Ask, "What events did you read about in this lesson that Paul could have used as excuses for discouragement?"

2. Read aloud 1 Thessalonians 2:19. Notice how Paul focused on that which was eternal instead of temporal. How did that eternal focus help his heart stay sincere?

3. What were the three primary things that caused pain in Paul's ministry?

4. What reasons for Paul's positive emotions are specifically noted in Part 4 (pp. 41)?

Applying the Truths to Life

Select interactive questions from this lesson to discuss as a group. Be careful to choose ones that are for open discussion, since some are intended for personal reflection only. Include some from each of the four parts of the lesson. Significant questions to include are #2 (p. 34), #9 (p. 37), #13 (p. 39), #16 (p. 42), and #17 (p. 42).

Since the focus of this lesson is on keeping discouragement from being permanent, give the group a practical step to take. Pass out 3x5 cards or small pieces of paper. Then lead the group in prayer, asking God to bring to your mind the people you know who may be discouraged right now. After prayer, instruct the group to write that person's name and use the card as a prayer reminder. Pray that God would help the members of the group, either individually or corporately, to be an encouragement to those people.

Ministering to One Another

Ask group members to relate some of the opportunities they've had to help bear the burden of someone else. (Their examples do not have to be about how they helped someone who is part of your group.) Next, talk about some specific things that members could do for others in the coming week.

Reaching Out to Others

If yours is an open group, did you set an empty chair in your circle? What will you do to fill it the next time you meet? Remember, if you do not plan for it, your group probably won't grow. In the closing prayer time, pray for people by name whom you will invite to the next group meeting.

Closing Prayer Time

Review your prayer sheets and ask for updates. Then allow members to share new prayer requests. Encourage members to be open with the group, but remind everyone of the importance of keeping confidences.

LESSON 4

The Morality of the Moment

1 Thessalonians 4:1–12

Look around and ask yourself this question: What is important to people today? Now take the various things that made your mental list and see how many of them can fit under one of the following two headings: sex and self.

Our world is dominated by sex. It is used in advertising to sell everything from motor oil to toothpaste. The displays in the window of a typical clothing store at the mall shout just one word, and it's *sex*. Entertainment features sexual themes, sexual overtones, sexual undertone, and often just plain sex. Films and programs are labeled AC for adult content, SC for sexual content, N for nudity, PG-13, R, NC-17, and X, besides the vague listing MC for mature content. This is a sex-driven culture, one in which lust is constantly being fanned into flames. Why else would the most prominent usage of the Internet be to access pornographic Web sites?

▶ **1. What percentage of content on the Internet do you think is pornographic?**

☐ 25% ☐ 50% ☐ 75%

▶ **2. According to information posted at www.cwfa.org, "More than 80 percent of content on the Internet is pornographic." In five words or less, what is your reaction to this statistic?**

_____

_____

Now look for evidence of the drive to please self. How many credit card applications do you throw away each day? Easy credit can help you please yourself, to have what you want right now. How many commercials or advertisements do you see for investment services? They can help you have the life you want. Do you need a new car, or do you just want one with more features, more options, softer seats, classier styling, or more comforts? Having difficulty deciding what to eat?

45

Options abound so you can get what you want, how you want it, and when you want it. The service industry is out there, ready to serve you.

▶ **3. Define, either in your own words or using a dictionary, *materialism*.**
_____
_____
_____

▶ **4. Why does a desire to please self increase a person's materialistic thinking?**
_____
_____
_____

The more you look, the more evidence you will find that sex and self are among the salient features of our culture. These two dominate our cultural landscape. Sadly, the church is not making a significant impact on our society, as is evident in so many ways. Consider the entertainment industry. A quick glance at the advertisements for movies and television shows reveals an emphasis on and frequent inclusion of sexual themes. It's also obvious from advertising that much of what is sold is not to meet the basic necessities of life but to cater to our selfish desires.

When Paul and his two missionary companions entered the city of Thessalonica, they faced a philosophy of life that was very similar to our own today. Though they found a Jewish synagogue, the values of the Old Testament had made little difference to the Gentiles who lived in this pagan city. Furthermore, the Jews themselves had been so tainted and influenced by the Greek and Roman cultures that they had no clear-cut witness in this sinful society.

However, through the power of the Gospel and the regenerating work of the Holy Spirit, many of these people—both Jews and Gentiles—had been converted to Jesus Christ and a new way of life. In fact, Paul, Silas, and Timothy began immediately to teach these people how to live for Christ. "Finally, brothers, we instructed you how to live in order to please God, as in fact you are living" (4:1). Flowing out of this commendation of their ministry and encouragement to persevere comes a section of practical instruction that speaks directly to the subjects of sex and self, challenging us to be people who go against the flow of our world, to move forward in a backward world.

Lesson 4: The Morality of the Moment

PART 1: Interacting with the Scripture

Reading/Hearing God's Word

Read or Listen to:

☐ 1 Thessalonians 4:1–12

▶ 5. Using your Bible, read or listen to the passage of Scripture listed in the margin. As you begin, ask God to speak to you through His Word. Watch for verses or ideas that are especially meaningful to you today. Once you finish, check the box indicating that you have read the passage.

Meditating on God's Word

▶ 6. Write a brief summary of a meaningful verse or idea you noticed.

_____

_____

_____

Memorizing God's Word

▶ 7. During the time you are studying this lesson, commit to memory 1 Thessalonians 4:7. Memorizing this key verse will help you remember the important points of this lesson.

Understanding God's Word

1 Thessalonians 4:3–7

³"It is God's will that you should be sanctified: that you should avoid sexual immorality; ⁴ that each of you should learn to control his own body in a way that is holy and honorable, ⁵ not in passionate lust like the heathen, who do not know God; ⁶ and that in this matter no one should wrong his brother or take advantage of him. The Lord will punish men for all such sins, as we have already told you and warned you. ⁷ For God did not call us to be impure, but to live a holy life."

▶ 8. Read again the focal passage for this week's lesson (1 Thess. 4:3–7) in the margin. Underline any key phrases or ideas that seem especially meaningful to you.

▶ 9. Look back at these verses. Circle one of the underlined phrases or words that you would like to understand or experience more fully.

Looking through the Scripture to God

Now pause to pray. "God, help me to see the world as it is, saturated with sexuality and focused on self. Help me also see what You desire, and may it be my desire to please You in the way that I live. May my life reflect You, and may I be used to encourage others to be people of holiness."

A Standard of Conduct

Paul was never satisfied with the level of maturity either in his own life or in the lives of other believers. Therefore, he went on to say, "Now we ask you and urge you in the Lord Jesus to do this more and more" (4:1). This was instruction on how they were to live their daily lives as the people of God. This is to be the standard of conduct for all of God's people all of the time. By living this way, we will please God.

Furthermore, Paul reminded them that the instructions he, Silas, and Timothy had given these people regarding living a Christian lifestyle were not based on their own viewpoint and convictions. Rather, he said, "You know what instructions we gave you by the authority of the Lord Jesus" (v. 2). What follows, then, is not a human point of view but God's. Any arguments or resistance to this teaching must be recognized as a disagreement with Almighty God, who has said on numerous occasions, "Be holy as I am holy." And so it is with any Christian in the 21st century. The specific areas addressed in this section are holiness and harmony, which fall under the categories of sex and self.

▶ 10. How do the following shape the morality of our culture?

• TV

_____

• movies

_____

• lifestyles of famous people

_____

• talk shows

_____

• the Bible

_____

PART 2: Ministry Today Requires Holiness (4:3–8)

Paul makes immediately clear in this paragraph that holiness is identified—indeed, is synonymous—with sexual purity. The words "It is God's will" (v. 3) move what follows out of the sphere of suggestion or encouragement to command. In verses 3 and 4, Paul issues a three-part command.

Lesson 4: The Morality of the Moment

The Command (vv. 3–4)

> **1 Thessalonians 4:3–4**
>
> "It is God's will that you should be sanctified: that you should avoid sexual immorality; that each of you should learn to control his own body in a way that is holy and honorable."

Be sanctified. The essential meaning of *sanctified* is "to be set apart." We are to be set apart to God. This involves a progressive holiness of life. It is progressive in the sense that we are continually in need of growing in godliness and holiness. None of us has arrived yet. At the same time there is a completed aspect to our sanctification. Our position in heaven is that of one who has been sanctified.

However, we are not to rest in the fact that we are viewed as sanctified in heaven. Instead, we are to continue to work on our lives, considering carefully how God would have us live, to progress in holy living. Simply stated, we are to keep becoming more like Jesus.

▶ 11. What specific things can you do to progress in holy living?

_____

_____

_____

Avoid sexual immorality. Extramarital sexual relations were accepted as the norm in the pagan culture of New Testament times. Ceremonial prostitution was part of the religious system. Fornication and adultery were common practices.

Men, particularly, took sexual liberties with women other than their wives. Often a slave owner would have sexual relations with a slave girl on a regular basis because she was accessible to him in the same home he shared with his legal spouse. Wives, of course, knew all about their husbands' sexual behavior. However, because they could do little, if anything, about the behavior, they accepted these practices as part of life. They had no other options open to them before the arrival of the Christian Gospel.

> **Exodus 20:14, 17**
>
> "'You shall not commit adultery. . . . You shall not covet your neighbor's house. You shall not covet your neighbor's wife, or his manservant or maidservant, his ox or donkey, or anything that belongs to your neighbor.'"

The message of Christianity brought with it a whole new point of view to those caught up in this licentious lifestyle. The message was one of sexual purity—a reiteration, of course, of the laws God had given to Israel years before (see Exodus 20:14, 17 in the margin).

And in reiterating God's laws, Paul contrasted Christ's message of holiness with the pagan world. A Christian must not give in to "passionate lust like the heathen, who do not know God" (v. 5). Holiness and sexual immorality are mutually exclusive.

▶ 12. Read Proverbs 5 and 6:20–35. List specific things to do to maintain sexual purity.

_____

_____

_____

Control yourself. Flowing out of the first two aspects of this command is the necessary course of action for the believer: control. This is how a person avoids sexual immorality. Christians are not victims of circumstances or of their passions. These desires can and must be controlled. We are not immune to temptation, but we are to resist it.

▶ 13. "Back of every tragedy in human character lies a long history of wicked thinking" (Bob Jones Sr.). How does this quote illustrate Proverbs 6:23–25 (in the margin)?

_____

_____

_____

The similarity between now and then is obvious. Moral standards are generally very low. Purity is regarded by some as an unrealistic expectation. But God's standard is clear and uncompromising.

The Contrast with the World (v. 5)

There is a resulting contrast. As believers live a life of sexual purity and control, the difference between them and those who are not followers of Christ becomes increasingly obvious. Instead of being controlled by knowing God, they are controlled by passionate lust. The Christian is to be different. Purity and control are part of the holiness required of us.

The Concern for a Brother (v. 6)

Sexual sin is not sin against God alone. In a stricter sense, sexual sin is certainly a sin against our brothers and sisters in Christ. But here Paul indicates that sexual sin is sin against any person who participates in sinful activities. People who engage in illicit sexual relations are sinning against each other. "In this matter," Paul wrote, "no one should wrong his brother or take advantage of him" (v. 6).

Proverbs 6:23–25

"For these commands are a lamp, this teaching is a light, and the corrections of discipline are the way to life, keeping you from the immoral woman, from the smooth tongue of the wayward wife. Do not lust in your heart after her beauty or let her captivate you with her eyes."

The Consequences of Immorality (vv. 6b–8)

God will ultimately judge sexual sin. While with them in Thessalonica, Paul had emphasized this point and warned these new Christians against continuing in their old practices (v. 6b). Note that Paul was not condemning sex per se. Over the years some well-meaning Christians have found it very difficult to differentiate between legitimate sex and illegitimate sex. Some have even classified the original sin as a sexual sin! This view is wrong, for the Bible presents sex as God-created, a means for procreation, and a marvelous expression of love.

At the time of his visit, Paul was teaching against improper sexual expression—sexual relations outside the bonds of marriage. Within God's scheme of things, the adulterer and those involved in sexual immorality will be judged (see Hebrews 13:4 in the margin).

Hebrews 13:4

"Marriage should be honored by all, and the marriage bed kept pure, for God will judge the adulterer and all the sexually immoral."

▶ **14. As far as your sexual purity, is God pleased with you, or is there a need for change in your thinking, your behavior, your relationships?**

_____

_____

_____

PART 3: Ministry Today Requires Harmony (4:9–12)

In the previous passage Paul told the Thessalonians that it was God's will that they should live a life of holiness (vv. 3–8). Now, in verses 9–12, he addresses God's will for them to live a life of love. As Warren Wiersbe stated it so well, the issues of Thessalonians 4 are holiness and harmony.[1]

We must go from a life of lust to a life of love. Love is to be lived.

The second dominant feature of our cultural landscape is self. The call to holiness moves forward to God's ideal, against the backward trend of our world to what appeals to man. Addressing the subject of love, Paul's teaching counters the emphasis on self, commanding us to think instead of others and strive for harmony.

▶ **15. What are some ways that selfish behavior can destroy relationships?**

_____

_____

_____

Again Paul commended the Thessalonians for their response to his teaching. In fact, they had continued to grow in brotherly love even after Paul, Silas, and Timothy had left them.

But again, Paul was not satisfied. He made it clear that none of us as Christians has or ever will love others as Christ has loved us. Therefore, Christ's love should be a constant goal. So Paul again challenged them with these words, "Yet we urge you, brothers, to do so [love the brothers] more and more" (v. 10).

The hallmark of true Christian maturity among Christians is sexual purity and brotherly love. These two concepts, of course, are not unrelated. True love for a brother and sister in Christ—outside of our marriage partner—should not be sexual. Though it involves a deep sense of friendship, affectionate feelings, and unselfish caring, it must never involve sexual stimulation.

▶ **16. Do not move on in this study until you understand clearly that sexual immorality is never true love.**

Love (vv. 9–10)

At this point it is important to understand God's total perspective on love. There are two Greek words used in the New Testament for love. Paul used both in these two verses. The word used most frequently in the New Testament is *agapao*, or agape love. Paul used this word twice in verses 9 and 10. In most instances New Testament writers used *agape* to portray loving acts—that is, behaving in certain ways because it is the right thing to do. This is the love defined in 1 Corinthians 13.

▶ **17. First Corinthians 13:6 says, "Love does not delight in evil." Why is that a characteristic of love?**

_____

_____

_____

Another word used in the Greek New Testament for love is *philos*. Though it is used interchangeably at times with *agapao*, it seemingly also has a distinctive meaning. It is associated with true friendship. Perhaps one of the best definitions of this kind of love is "a deep emotional feeling of trust generated from one person to another person."[2]

1 Thessalonians 4:9–10

"Now about brotherly love we do not need to write to you, for you yourselves have been taught by God to love each other. And in fact, you do love all the brothers throughout Macedonia. Yet we urge you, brothers, to do so more and more."

> **Romans 12:9–10**
>
> "Love must be sincere. Hate what is evil; cling to what is good. Be devoted to one another in brotherly love. Honor one another above yourselves."
>
> **1 Peter 1:22**
>
> "Now that you have purified yourselves by obeying the truth so that you have sincere love for your brothers, love one another deeply, from the heart."
>
> **2 Peter 1:7**
>
> "And to godliness, brotherly kindness; and to brotherly kindness, love."
>
> **1 Thessalonians 4:11–12**
>
> "Make it your ambition to lead a quiet life, to mind your own business and to work with your hands, just as we told you, so that your daily life may win the respect of outsiders and so that you will not be dependent on anybody."

In writing to the Thessalonians, Paul made reference to this kind of love. The Greek word translated "brotherly love," which Paul used in verse 9, is the word *philadelphia* (from *philos*, "love," and *delphos*, "brothers"). In context it is clear that Paul was referring to the loving, sensitive, and caring relationships that should exist between brothers and sisters in Jesus Christ. The Thessalonian Christians had already excelled in this kind of love.

Paul said he did not need to write to them about brotherly love because they already had been taught about and practiced agape love (v. 9). It is not unusual to find *agape* and *philos* in the same verse (see Romans 12:9–10, 1 Peter 1:22, and 2 Peter 1:7 in the margin). If we "agape" one another, we will have "philadelphia." This was the situation in Thessalonica.

In spite of the positive words he has to say about their love for one another, Paul again says, "Yet we urge you, brothers, to do so more and more" (v. 10). There was still room for improvement. Most of us fit in this category. We may have been instructed in agape love and even practice phileo love, but still we need to do better.

What follows next is an unfortunate paragraph break. Verses 9–12 should be kept together. Verse 11 begins in the Greek with the word *and*. Having said that they needed to keep working on their brotherly love, Paul next gives them three very specific examples for how this love is to be lived.

Lived (vv. 11–12)

Lead a restful life. Was it difficult finding the time to participate in this study? Are you always on the lookout for a calendar that has larger spaces for writing in activities? Do you need a memory upgrade on your PDA to accommodate more items for your date book? Welcome to the rush of the 21st century. Paul was obviously in the first century; otherwise, he would have known better than to even suggest living a quiet life!

So stop for a moment, which may be hard. Listen to what Paul is saying. Living a quiet life is to be our "ambition" (v. 11). Next time you are reading through the Gospels, notice that Jesus never rushed anywhere. He was never in a hurry, nor was He late. He knew what God wanted Him to do, did it, and did not get off track or caught up in the pace of society.

It may seem a bit out of the flow of thought that Paul would deal with the pace of life while giving specific examples of how love is lived in the reality of life. Yet it does fit. He says that we are to improve on our love for others, and to do this means living a quiet life. Here is how the two fit together. Have you ever felt loved by a busy person? Probably not. And when you think you can be busy and still show love, remember your answer to that question. Just as you do not feel loved by a busy person, others do not feel loved by you if you are a busy person. God does not want us to live without time for relationships.

▶ **18.** "If the devil can't make you bad, he'll make you busy." How does that saying relate to these verses?

_____

_____

_____

With the next two examples, the issue of self is addressed in a very practical way. The person who lives for self, who puts self first, may well violate these.

Mind your own business. Now here's a novel idea for showing love! It probably does not need much explanation because the connection is obvious. Though one aspect of love is demonstrating concern and offering help to others, love is not to be confused with meddling or overstaying one's welcome (see Proverbs 25:17 in the margin). The command is clear: "mind your own business" (v. 11).

Be self-supporting. The Thessalonians evidently had a problem that resulted from a false view of the Second Coming of Christ. Some used this doctrine to justify not working, so they relied on others to meet their physical needs. Evidently they were rationalizing that since Christ was coming back to take them home to heaven, there was no need to make a living.

This problem did not go away easily for the Thessalonians. In fact, Paul picked up the same theme in his second letter (see 2 Thessalonians 3:11–12 in the margin). In fact, he became very direct in reminding them of something he and the others had taught these people when they were with them. "We gave you this rule: 'If a man will not work, he shall not eat'" (2 Thess. 3:10). Those who were not working depended on others instead of providing for themselves. Love will reach out to help those in need, but it is not love to intentionally create the need and wait for others to extend their love.

And Paul made it clear as to why he was concerned that they be diligent in making a living. He did not want their lifestyle to be a stumbling block to those who did not know Christ. Furthermore, he did not want them to take advantage of their brothers and sisters in Christ (v. 12).

There is to be harmony in the Body of Christ. It is not automatic, but it is expected. Paul's instruction is basic: we are to have agape love that manifests itself in phileo love. To make it clear, he gives us examples of how love is lived out in relationships with others. Our emphasis is on others, not self.

Proverbs 25:17

"Seldom set foot in your neighbor's house—too much of you, and he will hate you."

2 Thessalonians 3:11–12

"We hear that some among you are idle. They are not busy; they are busybodies. Such people we command and urge in the Lord Jesus Christ to settle down and earn the bread they eat."

Lesson 4: The Morality of the Moment

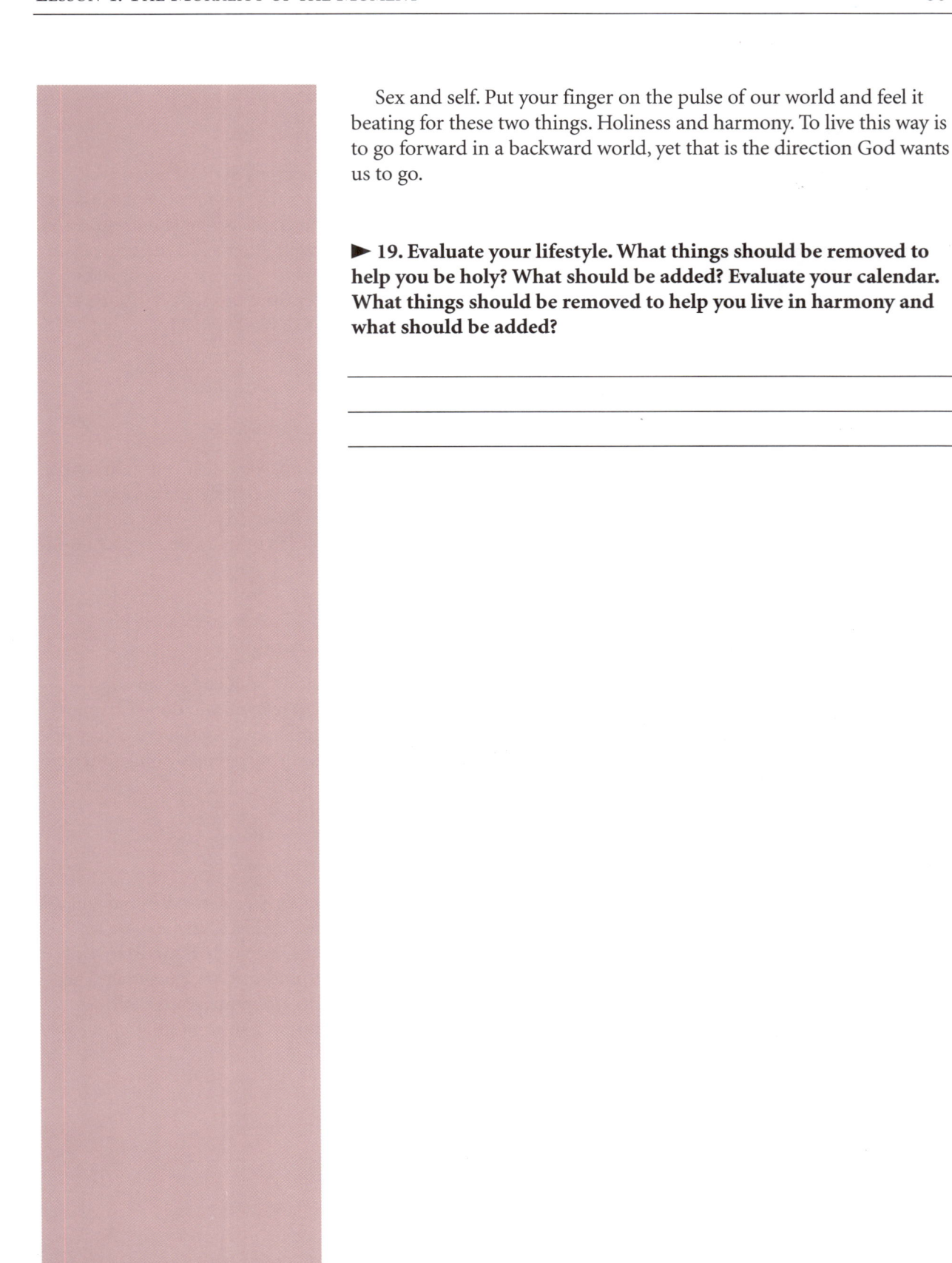

Sex and self. Put your finger on the pulse of our world and feel it beating for these two things. Holiness and harmony. To live this way is to go forward in a backward world, yet that is the direction God wants us to go.

▶ **19. Evaluate your lifestyle. What things should be removed to help you be holy? What should be added? Evaluate your calendar. What things should be removed to help you live in harmony and what should be added?**

_____

_____

_____

Small-Group Meeting 4

Opening Prayer

Begin your time together with prayer. Ask God to help you approach this lesson on purity with an open heart. Be willing to let the Holy Spirit make you aware of aspects of your life in which holiness is not as evident or real as God desires.

Building Relationships

Allow group members to share something from their journals. Perhaps an especially meaningful verse that they noted during the past week, a prayer that was answered, or a blessing they received.

Reviewing the Lesson

1. The introduction to this lesson quickly draws attention to how our culture is fixated on sex and self. Ask the group what safeguards they have to keep themselves from being seduced by Internet sites that feature pornography.

2. Discuss what holiness means. Is the common attitude toward holiness positive or negative? Is it perceived to be something desirable or not? Why?

3. Another word to define is *sanctification*. Perhaps someone has a study Bible with terms such as this defined. Or you may want to look it up before the group meets.

4. In Part 2 it says that "sexual sin is certainly a sin against our brothers and sisters in Christ" (p. 50). How is that true?

5. How does sexual immorality affect the harmony of the local church? How does holiness affect it?

6. Compare and contrast the two types of love mentioned in Part 3 (pp. 52-54). What specific examples did Paul give of how love is to be lived?

Applying the Truths to Life

Select interactive questions to discuss as a group. Be careful to choose ones that are for open discussion since some are intended for personal reflection and are not for sharing with others. Include some from each of the three parts of the lesson. Significant questions to consider from this lesson include #2 (p. 45), #10 (p. 48), #12 (p. 50), #17 (p. 52), and #18 (p. 54).

Ministering to One Another

Perhaps things are going well with you right now, but you need to remember Paul's admonition in 1 Corinthians 10:12. Read it again. How can you encourage and help each other to be people of holiness and harmony?

Reaching Out to Others

If yours is an open group, did you set an empty chair in your circle? What will you do to fill it next time you meet? Begin discussing the possibility of a couple of people from your group leading others through this same study.

Closing Prayer Time

Go through your prayer sheets item by item and ask for an update. Following this, share new prayer requests. Remind the group of the importance of keeping confidences, and then pray together. These prayer times will help group members discover opportunities to minister to one another.

LESSON 5

Taking a Load Off the Mind

1 Thessalonians 4:13–18

In his teaching about the resurrection, John MacArthur quotes an interesting description of death:

"There is a preacher of the old school, but he speaks as boldly as ever. He is not popular, though the world is his parish and he travels every part of the globe and speaks in every language. He visits the poor, calls upon the rich, preaches to people of every religion and no religion, and the subject of his sermon is always the same. He is an eloquent preacher, often stirring feelings which no other preacher could, and bringing tears to eyes that never weep. His arguments none are able to refute, nor is there any heart that has remained unmoved by the force of his appeals. He shatters life with his message. Most people hate him; everyone fears him. His name? Death. Every tombstone is his pulpit, every newspaper prints his text, and someday every one of you will be his sermon." [1]

We cannot escape the reality of death. The newspaper we read today, the cemetery we drive by on our way to the mall, the sound of the ambulance siren we hear late at night, and perhaps even the photographs of fondly remembered relatives hanging on our family room wall all remind of us the inevitability of death.

Losing a loved one is always painful. It's a time of deep sorrow and sadness—particularly if the death is sudden or premature, from a human point of view. And sometimes it raises questions we cannot answer completely. Death always brings questions, some of which are very difficult, perhaps impossible, to answer. But some we can answer—and with certainty!

So it was with the Thessalonian Christians. When Timothy returned from visiting this church, he related their questions about death to Paul. And in this passage Paul answers one of these questions: What happens to a Christian who dies before Christ comes again?

▶ **1. What are some basic questions people have about death?**

_____
_____
_____

▶ **2. What are some popular ideas about death? Do these ideas agree or disagree with the Bible?**

_____
_____
_____

2 Corinthians 5:6–8

"Therefore we are always confident and know that as long as we are at home in the body we are away from the Lord. We live by faith, not by sight. We are confident, I say, and would prefer to be away from the body and at home with the Lord."

There are two things regarding death that God does not want. One is that we be ignorant about those "who fall asleep" (1 Thess. 4:13). Death is often likened to sleep. For the Christian, the idea of sleeping in the arms of Jesus is a wonderful image of safety and comfort. Even the word *cemetery* means "a sleeping place." It is the place where our bodies sleep, awaiting the resurrection. Our souls do not sleep—they are with Jesus (see 2 Corinthians 5:6–8 in margin). God wants us to understand this.

The other thing God does not want is that we "grieve like the rest of men, who have no hope" (v. 13). The Bible assumes that we will grieve, and nowhere does Scripture belittle grief. What Paul is prohibiting here is hopeless grief, which would be like the grief of those who are not Christians.

Death does bring questions. In this passage, Paul gives insight into the experience that all of us face—death—and gives us hope.

PART 1: Interacting with the Scripture

Reading/Hearing God's Word

Read or Listen to:

☐ 1 Thessalonians 4:13–18

▶ **3. Using your Bible, read or listen to the passage of Scripture listed in the margin. As you begin, ask God to speak to you through His Word. Watch for verses or ideas that are especially meaningful to you today. Once you finish, check the box indicating that you have read the passage.**

LESSON 5: TAKING A LOAD OFF THE MIND   59

1 Thessalonians 4:13–18

¹³ "Brothers, we do not want you to be ignorant about those who fall asleep, or to grieve like the rest of men, who have no hope. ¹⁴ We believe that Jesus died and rose again and so we believe that God will bring with Jesus those who have fallen asleep in him.

¹⁵ "According to the Lord's own word, we tell you that we who are still alive, who are left till the coming of the Lord, will certainly not precede those who have fallen asleep. ¹⁶ For the Lord himself will come down from heaven, with a loud command, with the voice of the archangel and with the trumpet call of God, and the dead in Christ will rise first. ¹⁷ After that, we who are still alive and are left will be caught up together with them in the clouds to meet the Lord in the air. And so we will be with the Lord forever. ¹⁸ Therefore encourage each other with these words."

Meditating on God's Word

▶ 4. Write a brief summary of a meaningful verse or idea you noticed.

_____
_____
_____

Memorizing God's Word

▶ 5. During the time you are studying this lesson, commit to memory 1 Thessalonians 4:16–18. Memorizing these key verses will help you remember the important points of this lesson.

Understanding God's Word

▶ 6. Read again the focal passage for this week's lesson (1 Thess. 4:13–18) in the margin. Underline any key phrases or ideas that seem especially meaningful to you.

▶ 7. Look back at these verses. Circle one of the underlined phrases or words that you would like to understand or experience more fully.

Looking through the Scripture to God

Now pause to pray. "Death is real, Father. I know that, but there is much I do not know about death. Thank You for this passage, which has hope-giving instruction. Help me learn it well so that I will face death unafraid and know the comfort that You give in my times of sorrow."

PART 2: Christains Who Die Have Hope (4:14)

After Paul and his missionary companions had left Thessalonica, it appears that some of the Thessalonian believers died. Even though Paul had instructed the Thessalonians regarding the Second Coming of Christ, they still didn't understand some things. They understood that Christ was coming again. In fact, people everywhere were telling Paul, Silas, and Timothy how these people had "turned to God from idols to serve the living and true God, and to wait for his Son from heaven" (1:9–10). But they did not understand that Christ might not come immediately and that, in the meantime, some of their loved ones would die. What would happen to them?

The answer to this question seems obvious to us. But we must remember that many of these people were converted from idolatry. The idea of a personal Savior who would return to take them home to heaven was radical. That marvelous truth helps explain why some of them stopped working and decided to wait for Jesus Christ to deliver them from their difficult situation on earth (4:11–12).

Paul's answer to the question was that all Christians have hope—whether we live or die! Therefore, he continued, "We believe that Jesus died and rose again and so we believe that God will bring with Jesus those who have fallen asleep in him" (v. 14). For Christians, relief from sorrow is found in what the future holds.

John 14:1–3

"'Do not let your hearts be troubled. Trust in God; trust also in me. In my Father's house are many rooms; if it were not so, I would have told you. I am going there to prepare a place for you. And if I go and prepare a place for you, I will come back and take you to be with me that you also may be where I am.'"

▶ **8. Read John 14:1–3 in the margin. How did Jesus calm the troubled hearts of His disciples?**

_____

_____

_____

At this point Paul begins to explain a wonderful truth. Those who die go immediately to be with Jesus Christ. This is why he wrote to the Corinthians that "to be away from the body" is to be "at home with the Lord" (2 Cor. 5:8).

True, the body remains on earth and soon decays and returns to dust. But the spirit goes to be with the Lord. This is why Stephen, who was dying at the hands of cruel men, cried out, "Lord Jesus, receive my spirit" (Acts 7:59). This is also why Jesus could turn to the thief on the cross, who in those final minutes placed his faith in Him, and say, "I tell you the truth, today you will be with me in paradise" (Luke 23:43). Obviously, that converted criminal's body went into a tomb, but his spirit—the real person—went to heaven to be with Christ.

1 Corinthians 15:42

"So will it be with the resurrection of the dead. The body that is sown is perishable, it is raised imperishable."

Paul made another point clear in verse 14. When Jesus comes again, those who have already died will come with Him when He returns. At that moment the old body will be resurrected as a new body. Writing to the Corinthians, Paul said that the dead will be "raised imperishable" (see 1 Corinthians 15:42 in the margin).

And let us not be concerned with such questions as how this can happen when a body has been cremated and scattered in the wind. If God can save us and give us a body that will never perish when He comes again, He can certainly handle the problem of burial and what happens to our dust.

▶ **9. How does 1 Corinthians 15:42 help you cope with aches and pains?**

_____

_____

_____

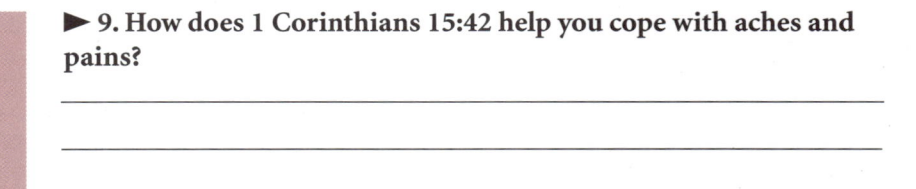

Because of Christ's Resurrection

There is no uncertainty in regard to our hope. "We believe . . . ," Paul wrote. While some translations make it sound uncertain, the construction in the Greek is factual. It could be translated, "Since we believe . . ." Our belief is "that Jesus died and rose again."

While the Christian takes comfort in describing death as "sleep," Paul does not speak of Christ sleeping but actually dying. Jesus faced the horror of death, which is the result of sin. He bore in His death the wages of sin, enduring the worst that death could possibly do. Because there was no mitigation of the horror of death for Him, there is no horror in death for His people. For them it is but sleep. We must remember, though, that our hope is based on the truth of Christ's resurrection. Yes, He died, and yes, He lives!

Because They Will Be United with Their Savior at His Coming

Three different Greek words are used to identify specific aspects of the return of Christ. The word *epiphania* means an appearing or a showing or a manifestation of Christ. Our English word *epiphany* is derived from it. *Apocalypse* comes from *apokalupsis*, which means an unveiling, a revelation. The other word, *parousia*, emphasizes Christ's physical presence and means "being alongside of," "the physical arrival of a ruler." It is used 15 times in the New Testament in reference to Christ's return. In verse 15 Paul uses the word *parousia*.

The Christian knows that the death and resurrection of Jesus Christ did indeed take place. Of equal certainty, then, is this truth: when Jesus returns for His living saints, He will bring with Him the souls of believers who have died.

There is great comfort in this truth! Paul took for granted that Christians should face death not with despair but with hope—a hope in what God will do, grounded in what He has already done.

In his commentary on 1 Thessalonians, Michael W. Holmes writes, "One of my all-time favorite Peanuts cartoons involves a conversation between Lucy and Linus. Looking out a window, Lucy wonders: 'Boy, look at it rain . . . what if it floods the whole world?' 'It will never do that,' says Linus. 'In the ninth chapter of Genesis, God promised Noah that would never happen again, and the sign of the promise is the rainbow.' 'You've taken a great load off my mind,' replies Lucy, to which Linus responds: 'Sound theology has a way of doing that'!" [2]

That is what Paul was doing in this passage, offering "sound theology" as a comfort and encouragement to those trying to make sense of the universal human experience of death.

▶ **10. The assurance of heaven calms a troubled heart. Read John 20:10–18 below. Describe the emotions of Mary at the beginning and at the end of this passage. What made the difference?**

_____

_____

_____

John 20:10–18

"Then the disciples went back to their homes, but Mary stood outside the tomb crying. As she wept, she bent over to look into the tomb and saw two angels in white, seated where Jesus' body had been, one at the head and the other at the foot.

"They asked her, 'Woman, why are you crying?'

"'They have taken my Lord away,' she said, 'and I don't know where they have put him.' At this, she turned around and saw Jesus standing there, but she did not realize that it was Jesus.

"'Woman,' he said, 'why are you crying? Who is it you are looking for?'

"Thinking he was the gardener, she said, 'Sir, if you have carried him away, tell me where you have put him, and I will get him.'

"Jesus said to her, 'Mary.'

"She turned toward him and cried out in Aramaic, 'Rabboni!' (which means Teacher).

"Jesus said, 'Do not hold on to me, for I have not yet returned to the Father. Go instead to my brothers and tell them, "I am returning to my Father and your Father, to my God and your God."'

"Mary Magdalene went to the disciples with the news: 'I have seen the Lord!' And she told them that he had said these things to her."

Lesson 5: Taking a Load Off the Mind

PART 3: Christians Who Live Have Hope (4:15–17)

Paul emphasizes in this next section that "we who are still alive, who are left till the coming of the Lord, will certainly not precede those who have fallen asleep" (v. 15). Though we have hope and will be taken to heaven when Christ returns, our hope will not be greater than those who have died prior to this great event. Paul explains why this is true and how it will actually happen.

This is according to the Lord's own word. It is not a scheme of man or some wishful thinking. It is the truth from God and it gives us hope. We live expecting the parousia, the coming of Christ, because it could be today.

The Return of Christ (v. 16)

What Paul now describes is not to be confused with the Second Coming, or Christ's return to the earth. This instead is the event referred to as the Rapture. In the Latin translation of verse 17 the word *rapturo* was used to translate the Greek word *harpazo*, which means "to snatch or take away." This is the classic passage on the Rapture of the Church. It was written to instruct the Thessalonians regarding what would happen to believers who had died.

The One who will come at the end of this age is no less than "the Lord himself" (v. 16). The word translated "loud command" often denotes an authoritative utterance. It is the cry made by the ship's master to his rowers, or by a military officer to his soldiers, or by a hunter to his hounds, or by a charioteer to his horses. When used by military or naval personnel it was a battle cry.

There will also be the voice of an archangel and the trumpet call of God. Trumpets are often mentioned in the Old Testament in connection with times of festivity and triumph. They were a frequent accompaniment of great religious occasions. Jesus speaks of the trumpet in connection with the parousia (see Matthew 24:31 in the margin.)

At this moment, "the dead in Christ will rise first. After that," Paul continues, "we who are still alive and are left will be caught up together with them in the clouds to meet the Lord in the air. And so we will be with the Lord forever" (vv. 16–17).

Bodily Resurrection (v. 16)

In answering this question, "What happens to a Christian who dies before Christ comes again?" Paul makes it perfectly clear that both those who die in Christ and those who are alive in Christ will be of equal status when He comes. The "dead in Christ" are believers who have died since the Day of Pentecost. At the Rapture, their glorified bodies will be

---

Matthew 24:31

"'And he will send his angels with a loud trumpet call, and they will gather his elect from the four winds, from one end of the heavens to the other.'"

resurrected and rejoined with their souls, which had been in heaven with Christ, and then those who are alive will follow.

The Rapture (v. 17)

The living saints will be caught up, or raptured, "to meet the Lord in the air" (v. 17). What Jesus said to His disciples then will find its ultimate fulfillment: He will come and receive them unto Himself (see John 14:1–3 in the margin on page 60).

▶ **11. When will the Rapture take place? Since we do not know the answer to that question, here is another one. When could the Rapture take place?**

_____
_____

▶ **12. You know how embarrassing it can be to have unexpected company come to your house when it is messy. Similarly, if Jesus were to come right now, what do you wish would be different in your life?**

_____
_____
_____

A Reunion (v. 17)

And then there will be a glorious reunion! One great host will be swept up into the air to meet Jesus. That means that if Christ came this very moment, those loved ones of ours who died in Him will be right there with us—maybe by our side! We'll both have new bodies—glorified bodies—that will never again deteriorate.

▶ **13. Are there some people you would like to see at that reunion but have not yet received Christ? Take time right now to pray for their salvation.**

The primary purpose of this passage is not to teach a scheme of prophecy but to comfort and encourage Christians whose loved ones have died. The comfort is based on the following: 1) the dead will be resurrected and will participate in the Lord's coming for His own; 2) when Christ comes the living will be reunited forever with their loved ones; and 3) they all will be with the Lord eternally. Remember the two things that God does not want—that we be ignorant regarding death or that we sorrow like those who do not have hope. Because of Scripture, we cannot be ignorant, and because of the resurrection of Jesus, our sorrow is different.

PART 4: Our Hope Is an Encouraging Hope (4:18)

Paul concludes this section of his letter with an exhortation: "Therefore encourage each other with these words" (v. 18).

▶ **14. God is equipping you to serve Him and help others who are grieving. How can you use these words to encourage others?**

_____

_____

_____

Today we know far more about God's great scheme of things because of His completed revelation in the Bible. Still, unanswered questions remain because God doesn't want us to know everything about the future. In fact, Jesus said, "No one knows about that day or hour, not even the angels in heaven, nor the Son, but only the Father" (Matt. 24:36). Therefore, it is inappropriate to set dates, as some Christians have tried to do through the years. But one thing we know—Jesus could come at any moment. Paul thought Christ would come in his lifetime. What about our lifetime—nearly 2,000 years later?

The main point Paul was making about the Lord's return is that for Christians it will be a glorious day, whether we are alive or dead when it happens. Even more important, Paul was writing to encourage Christians whose loved ones had died in Christ. We should be encouraged for at least three reasons.

Death for the Believer Is Like Sleep

Sleep is a familiar euphemism for death in the New Testament. Jesus said of Jairus's daughter, "She is not dead but asleep" (Luke 8:52), and when Stephen died, Acts 7:60 says, "he fell asleep." The bodies they left behind were just their temporary, earthly shells—what Paul would call "tents" and at death appear to be sleeping (see 2 Corinthians 5:1 in the

2 Corinthians 5:1

"Now we know that if the earthly tent we live in is destroyed, we have a building from God, an eternal house in heaven, not built by human hands."

margins). In reality, their spirits are in a conscious state with Jesus and will one day be reunited with their bodies, which will be changed by the resurrection power of Christ. So we look at death with this perspective—they are asleep in Jesus, they are with Jesus. Our loved ones who have died in Christ are actually alive with Jesus.

A Heavenly Reunion Awaits

The hardest thing about death is separation from our loved ones; but when Christ comes, we will be "with the Lord forever" (v. 17)! We'll see them again. We'll be reunited, not only in heaven but on the way up! Those Christians who were alive and well in Thessalonica had nothing to be concerned about. Their loved ones who had died were safe in the arms of Jesus. Someday they would be together again, rejoicing in the presence of God. And so it will be someday for all of us as believers.

Eternal Blessing Is Ours

We will be forever with the Lord. In a world heedless at best and hostile at worst, these are words of comfort. Paul told the Thessalonian Christians to "encourage each other with these words." Paul was not denying that there would be sorrow over the death of loved ones. Rather, he was telling them that their grief was different. Their separation was only temporary. They would be reunited again when Jesus Christ comes to take all His children home to heaven—those who have died and those who are still alive.

Many pastors have stood by open graves preaching funeral sermons for Christians who have lost loved ones. Again and again they have shared this basic message of encouragement. One of the most rewarding experiences a pastor can have is to be able to see joy expressed through tears. How tragic for those ministers who can eulogize but have nothing to say about eternity.

In 1963 four young girls were killed by a racist's bomb in Birmingham, Alabama. At their funeral, Dr. Martin Luther King said the following:

> I hope you can find some consolation from Christianity's affirmation that death is not the end. Death is not a period that ends the great sentence of life, but a comma that punctuates it to more lofty significance. Death is not a blind alley that leads the human race into a state of nothingness, but an open door which leads man into life eternal. Let this daring faith, this great invincible surmise, be your sustaining power during these trying days.[3]

Songwriter Bill Gaither put it this way:

> Because He lives I can face tomorrow,
> Because He lives all fear is gone;
> Because I know He holds the future.
> And life is worth the living just because He lives.[4]

All of this leads to some very important questions. What about your personal relationship with Jesus Christ? Do you know Him? Have you received Him? Do you have this hope? Do your children have this hope?

▶ **15. Do not conclude this study without answering this question: If Jesus came right now, would you be ready? Have you received Him as your Savior?**

You can have this hope by receiving Jesus Christ as your personal Savior, just as the Thessalonians did when Paul, Silas, and Timothy first came to that pagan city preaching the Gospel of Christ's death and resurrection.

Receive Him today and be ready. You have no assurance that you'll live another moment on this earth. You could die before you finish reading this paragraph. Furthermore, you have no assurance that Christ might not come this very moment—also before you finish reading this paragraph. Whether you die or whether you remain alive, you can—you should—be ready! Receive Jesus Christ today.

Small-Group Meeting 5

Opening Prayer

As you begin your time together, pray with special emphasis on the need to be prepared to meet the Lord either through death or through the Rapture. Ask God to help you approach this lesson on death with a heart open to learn what the Bible teaches regarding this seemingly unpleasant reality.

Building Relationships

Allow time for every group member to share one thing for which they praise God.

Reviewing the Lesson

1. Ask the group to share some of the questions they have about death. Remind them that not all of their questions will be answered during this study.

2. First Thessalonians 4:13 speaks of those who have no hope. Verse 14 describes our hope. Read verse 14 aloud. Ask, "Why does this verse encourage us when we are in sorrow?" Also ask, "Does this passage teach us that it is a sin to sorrow when someone dies?"

3. What are the four things found in 1 Thessalonians 4:15–17 that give us hope (pp. 63-64)?

4. First Thessalonians 4:18 says that we are to use these words to encourage each other. On the basis of these verses studied, what exactly should you say to a grieving person?

Applying the Truths to Life

Select interactive questions to discuss as a group. Be careful to choose ones that are for open discussion, since some are intended for personal reflection only. Include some from each of the four parts of the lesson. Significant questions to consider from this lesson include #2 (p. 58), #8 (p. 60), #10 (p. 62), and #14 (p. 65).

Ministering to One Another

Review activities that individuals or the group as a whole have done to encourage one another. This study has just three more lessons. Challenge the group not to stop helping others when the study is done.

Reaching Out to Others

If yours is an open group, did you set an empty chair in your circle? It is not too late to invite someone. Perhaps they, along with some others from this group, would begin a new group to study this book together. Ask members of the group to consider leading another study.

Closing Prayer Time

Looking at your prayer sheets, ask for an update on each item. Then allow members time to mention new prayer requests. Remind everyone of the importance of keeping confidences, and pray as a group for the needs that are mentioned.

LESSON 6

Staying Ready Till Quittin' Time

1 Thessalonians 5:1–11

After graduating from high school, Chuck Swindoll worked in a machine shop in Houston's industrial district for four and a half years. During the day he was an apprentice, learning the machinist trade, while at night he attended classes at the University of Houston. In his book *Rise and Shine*, he writes, "I often recall several unforgettable characters I met during those days." He tells about one man he calls "Tex," whom he describes in his inimitable way: "Tex had spent most of his adult life operating a turret lathe in the same shop. He was your typical machinist. He wore a little gray-and-white striped cap—always greasy—and overalls that needed an oil change." He then shares this story:

"When you work in a machine shop, your life revolves around a whistle. After punching the clock when you arrive, your work begins with a whistle. As lunch time arrives, it is announced by the same shrill sound. When your shift ends, there is yet another blast.

"Shoptalk for that final whistle is 'quittin' time.'

"Tex had worked so long in a machine shop, he had a kind of invisible sensor down inside. He seldom had to look at the clock. Somehow he always knew when it was getting close to that last whistle. I cannot recall his ever being caught short. Without fail, Tex was all washed up and ready to punch out a couple of minutes before the whistle blew.

"On one occasion I said to him, 'Well, Tex, it's about time to start gettin' ready for quittin' time.'

"I will never forget his response. In that slow Texas drawl, he said, 'Listen, boy . . . I stay ready to keep from gettin' ready for quittin' time.' It was his way of saying, 'That final whistle won't ever catch me unaware.'"

That answer comes to mind when Swindoll thinks about the Lord coming back, and then he says, "There are times I wonder how many will be caught off guard." [1]

▶ 1. What are some situations in which you might find yourself "caught off guard" if Jesus were to return right then?

_____
_____
_____

One of these days, your life on this earth will come to an end. It will be "quittin' time." Will you be ready?

One of Paul's concerns for the believers in the church at Thessalonica was that they were not ready. In this passage from 1 Thessalonians 5, he challenges us to be ready and tells us what that involves.

PART 1: Interacting with the Scripture

Reading/Hearing God's Word

▶ 2. Using your Bible, read or listen to the passage of Scripture listed in the margin. As you begin, ask God to speak to you through His Word. Watch for verses or ideas that are especially meaningful to you today. Once you finish, check the box indicating that you have read the passage.

Meditating on God's Word

▶ 3. Write a brief summary of a meaningful verse or idea you noticed.

_____
_____
_____

Memorizing God's Word

▶ 4. During the time you are studying this lesson, commit to memory 1 Thessalonians 5:5–6 (in the margin). Memorizing these key verses will help you remember the important points of this lesson.

Understanding God's Word

▶ 5. Read again the focal passage for this week's lesson (1 Thess. 5:1–4) in the margin. Underline any key phrases or ideas that seem especially meaningful to you.

Read or Listen to:

☐ 1 Thessalonians 5:1–11

1 Thessalonians 5:5–6

"You are all sons of the light and sons of the day. We do not belong to the night or to the darkness. So then, let us not be like others, who are asleep, but let us be alert and self-controlled."

1 Thessalonians 5:1–4

"Now, brothers, about times and dates we do not need to write to you, for you know very well that the day of the Lord will come like a thief in the night. While people are saying, 'Peace and safety,' destruction will come on them suddenly, as labor pains on a pregnant woman, and they will not escape.

"But you, brothers, are not in darkness so that this day should surprise you like a thief."

Lesson 6: Staying Ready Till Quittin' Time   71

▶ 6. Look back at these verses. Circle one of the underlined phrases or words that you would like to understand or experience more fully.

Looking through the Scripture to God

Now pause to pray: "Lord, help me to be ready for Your return. It is so easy for me to relax and not even think about the possibility that Jesus could come for me today. I need to be watchful and prepared. May this lesson encourage me to live ready."

A Solemn Warning

The joyful hope of the believer is found in 1 Thessalonians 4:13–18. But Paul follows that passage with a solemn warning that centers on the themes of personal watchfulness and constant preparedness. Building off his teaching on the Rapture, Paul takes the subject of the Lord's appearing and applies it to the lives of his readers. His purpose was not just to inform the people of things to come but to encourage them to live holy lives, even in the midst of their pagan surroundings.

PART 2: The Suddenness of God's Judgment (5:1–3)

1 Thessalonians 5:1–2

"Now, brothers, about times and dates we do not need to write to you, for you know very well that the day of the Lord will come like a thief in the night."

The Thessalonian Christians were already well aware that Christ was going to come again. Paul affirmed this again as he began chapter 5 (see 1 Thessalonians 5:1–2 in the margin). But the Thessalonian Christians were confused concerning certain details. That should not surprise us. Although we have God's complete written revelation in the Bible, it is still easy to be confused regarding certain aspects of this great event. One reason is that God has purposely not unveiled everything to us. But certain things He has made very clear—and these we need to understand.

▶ 7. What sources do people consult to know the future?

_____
_____

The only certain source is the Bible. How can we keep from being misled by those who claim to be able to tell the future?

_____
_____
_____

In the previous chapter, Paul, inspired by the Holy Spirit, clarified the issue of what happens to Christians who die before Christ returns. They and those who are still alive at this time "will be caught up . . . to meet the Lord in the air." Furthermore, Paul said, "We will be with the Lord forever" (4:17).

But what will happen next? These are the events Paul reviewed for the Thessalonians in this opening paragraph in chapter 5. He deals first with God's judgment on those people who will be alive when Christ returns but who are not true believers in the Lord Jesus Christ.

Note that Paul refers to "times and dates" (v. 1). This can best be translated "times and seasons." He was not writing about actual 24-hour days or specific dates. Rather, he meant periods of time when certain events will take place. This is an important distinction, because some well-meaning followers of Christ over the years have attempted to set specific dates. It is dangerous to set dates, even as some are doing today. "Well-meaning people have tried to set dates for our Lord's return, only to be embarrassed by their failures. However, it is possible to expect His coming without setting a specific time. No 'signs' must be fulfilled before He can return for His church." [2]

▶ **8. What "signs" must be fulfilled before Jesus can return for His Church?**

_____

_____

▶ **9. If we really believe that Jesus could return right now, how should that affect the way we live?**

_____

_____

_____

Another concept that needs clarification in the minds of many Christians today is what the authors of Scripture meant by the phrase "the day of the Lord." In this passage, Paul was not referring to a specific 24-hour day. Rather, he was speaking of a time period mentioned by many Old Testament prophets, such as Zechariah, who prophesied of a time when the Lord would judge the world and restore His chosen people (see Zechariah 1:14–16 in the margin).

Zechariah 1:14–16

"Then the angel who was speaking to me said, 'Proclaim this word: This is what the Lord Almighty says: "I am very jealous for Jerusalem and Zion, but I am very angry with the nations that feel secure. I was only a little angry, but they added to the calamity."

"'Therefore, this is what the Lord says: "I will return to Jerusalem with mercy, and there my house will be rebuilt. And the measuring line will be stretched out over Jerusalem," declares the Lord Almighty.'"

> **Isaiah 13:9–11**
>
> "See, the day of the Lord is coming—a cruel day, with wrath and fierce anger—to make the land desolate and destroy the sinners within it. The stars of heaven and their constellations will not show their light. The rising sun will be darkened and the moon will not give its light. I will punish the world for its evil, the wicked for their sins. I will put an end to the arrogance of the haughty and will humble the pride of the ruthless."

It is clear that this Old Testament prophet was speaking of an extended period of time when God will judge the wicked directly and dramatically (see also Isaiah 13:9–11 in the margin). That time is in stark contrast to what many identify as the "day of grace." This is the time period we are living in today. God in a special way is revealing His grace. Many believe that the Day of the Lord will begin when all Christians are raptured or "caught up" to be with the Lord—the event described in 1 Thessalonians 4:13–18. It appears to be an extended period of time lasting more than 1,000 years—including a time of tribulation on the earth and the actual coming of Christ to the earth to set up His millennial reign. It will seemingly culminate with what is described in Revelation 20:11–15 as the Great White Throne Judgment.

The most important thing you need to know about the Day of the Lord is this: it will come suddenly. Believers sometimes live as if they will never give account for their lives, not realizing the suddenness of the coming judgment that Paul teaches.

Like a Thief in the Night (v. 2)

After stating that the "day of the Lord" will come, Paul illustrates how unexpected it will be—"like a thief in the night," he explains (v. 2). It is one thing to be robbed in broad daylight. It is quite another to be robbed at night when we are sleeping. When Christ comes, many will be "asleep"—that is, totally unaware of what is happening.

▶ 10. What can we do to "stay awake"?

_____
_____
_____

Like Labor Pains (v. 3)

Christ's return will also happen suddenly, as Paul states in this second illustration. "Destruction will come on them suddenly, as labor pains on a pregnant woman." Paul's emphasis with using this analogy is the suddenness, not the destructive aspects, of Christ's coming.

Given that the Lord's return will be unexpected and sudden, we must live like it could be today. Don't lose sight of this. At various times throughout church history, Jesus' sudden return has been taught with special emphasis. A few examples of this include when the Black Plague was devastating Europe, during Mussolini's reign in Italy, and during the Six Day War. It's interesting how people viewed current events as reinforcing the fact that Jesus could come then. Every generation has lived with the expectancy that His return could be today.

▶ **11. Give examples you know of that people claimed were "signs" of the Lord's coming. Did those events really affect the way people lived?**

_____

_____

_____

Peace and safety (*pax et securitas*) "was a popular slogan of the imperial Roman propaganda machine. The promise of peace and security was what Rome offered to those peoples who submitted (willingly or unwillingly) to Roman rule and military power; it was seen as Rome's gift to those it conquered, virtually equivalent to an offer of deliverance or salvation from turmoil and danger."[3]

As Michael W. Holmes wrote a few years ago, "The same slogan is no less appealing today in the tumultuous world of the late 20th century, where political, economic, and social turmoil leave many, many people with a deep longing for some degree of stability and safety. Even in the U.S., which in comparison with much of the rest of the world enjoys unprecedented levels of peace and security, there is a deep sense of unease and insecurity. Its massive military power cannot guarantee domestic security, as the terrorist bombings of the World Trade Center and the federal office building in Oklahoma City have demonstrated. Its massive economic power does not guarantee personal economic security, as waves of corporate 'down-sizing' and layoffs have shown.

"Marketers have not been slow to exploit the resulting anxiety. Investment firms promise financial security. Ads for dead bolt locks, personal protection devices, and gated communities promise personal security (a promise now even making its way into automobile advertising). Ads for various other products promise to secure our health or future in other ways.

"But from Paul's perspective, any and all such claims are illusory and deceptive."[4]

▶ **12. Why do you think some Christians believe that Jesus might return today but continue to live as if He will not?**

_____

_____

_____

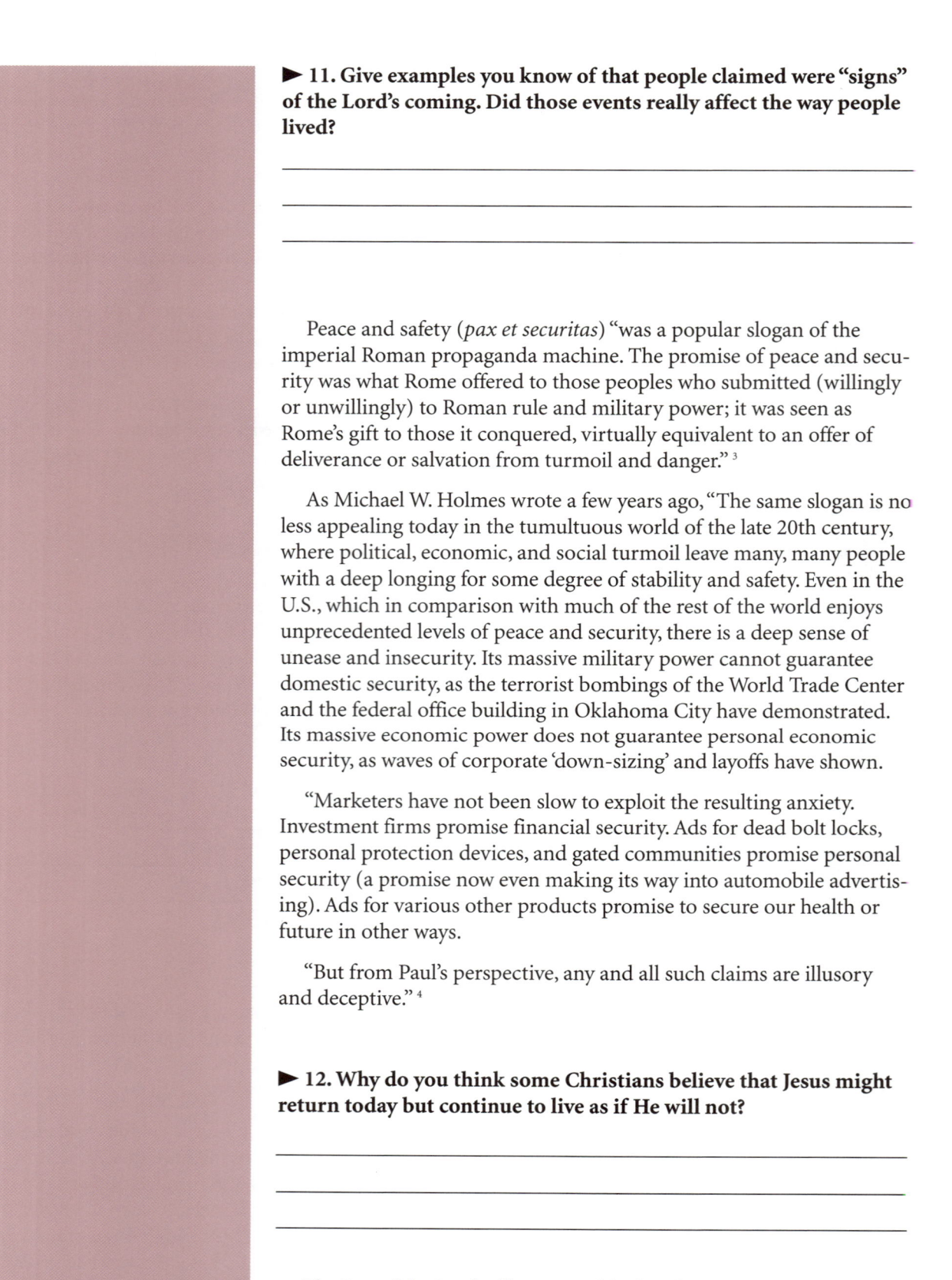

The Day of the Lord will come, suddenly. All is not hopeless. But there is a second application that follows close on the heels of this first one.

PART 3: We Should Not Be Caught by Surprise (5:4–5)

While verses 1–3 emphasize God's judgment on those who do not know Christ, the following ones emphasize that God will deliver from judgment those who are His children.

The word *rapture* is never used in the Bible. It means to be "caught up" and is described in 1 Thessalonians 4:15–17. Many believe this specific event will begin the time period identified as the Day of the Lord.

Views vary as to when the Rapture will occur. What Paul says in verses 9–10 of this chapter provide strong evidence to support the view that the Rapture will happen at the beginning of a seven-year tribulation period (see 1 Thessalonians 5:9–10 in the margin). During the Tribulation, God will pour out His wrath in judgment on mankind. These horrible judgments are described in detail in the Book of Revelation. But take heart. Christians will be in heaven during these events, for "God did not appoint us to suffer" this wrath that will be poured out upon the earth.

His Readers Were Not in the Dark (v. 4)

Those who know Jesus Christ as their personal Savior need not fear the Day of the Lord. Furthermore, this event should not take us by surprise. We are not "in darkness" (v. 4) concerning the return of Christ. We should constantly be looking for His coming. True, we should not set dates, but we should understand that it could happen at any moment. The world, however, will be caught by surprise because it will not hear God's Word or heed His warning.

His Readers Were Sons of the Light (v. 5)

Paul uses some very graphic words to describe those who will be taken to heaven when the Day of the Lord begins. They are "sons of the light"—not sons of the darkness. They are "sons of the day"—not sons of the night (v. 5).

Note how Paul describes this contrast in verses 4–5: "But you, brothers, are not in darkness so that this day should surprise you like a thief. You are all sons of the light and sons of the day. We do not belong to the night or to the darkness."

---

1 Thessalonians 5:9–10

"For God did not appoint us to suffer wrath but to receive salvation through our Lord Jesus Christ. He died for us so that, whether we are awake or asleep, we may live together with him. Therefore encourage one another and build each other up, just as in fact you are doing."

1 John 1:5–7

"This is the message we have heard from him and declare to you: God is light; in him there is no darkness at all. If we claim to have fellowship with him yet walk in the darkness, we lie and do not live by the truth. But if we walk in the light, as he is in the light, we have fellowship with one another, and the blood of Jesus, his Son, purifies us from all sin."

▶ **13. Read 1 John 1:5–7 in the margin. Do you think "walking in the light" is important? Why?**

_____

_____

_____

Consequently, we should constantly be looking for His coming. True, we should not set dates, but we should understand that it could happen at any moment.

There is a difference between being ready to go to heaven and being ready to meet the Lord. That's why Paul had one more piece of instruction for his readers concerning the Lord's return.

PART 4: Our Lives Should Be Characterized by Sobriety and Self-Control (5:6–11)

In view of the fact that Christ could come at any moment, Paul admonished the Thessalonian Christians—and us—to do several things. The previous teaching in this passage provides a solid basis for the ethical behavior he now urges.

Be Alert (v. 6b)

In verse 6, Paul contrasts alertness with being "asleep." As Christians, he says, we can become like non-Christians in our attitudes and actions. We can get so caught up in this world that we lose sight of our eternal destiny. The "sleep" Paul warns against is spiritual lethargy and insensitivity, and includes the inattention to spiritual priorities, which is utterly out of keeping for the believer.

▶ **14. Make a list of things that should be spiritual priorities in your life. Then compare it to the reality of your life.**

_____

_____

_____

This is particularly dangerous in the materialistic and entertainment-oriented world in which we live. Never before in the history of the world have we—particularly we Americans—had so many

LESSON 6: STAYING READY TILL QUITTIN' TIME

Ephesians 6:11–18

"Put on the full armor of God so that you can take your stand against the devil's schemes. For our struggle is not against flesh and blood, but against the rulers, against the authorities, against the powers of this dark world and against the spiritual forces of evil in the heavenly realms. Therefore put on the full armor of God, so that when the day of evil comes, you may be able to stand your ground, and after you have done everything, to stand. Stand firm then, with the belt of truth buckled around your waist, with the breastplate of righteousness in place, and with your feet fitted with the readiness that comes from the gospel of peace. In addition to all this, take up the shield of faith, with which you can extinguish all the flaming arrows of the evil one. Take the helmet of salvation and the sword of the Spirit, which is the word of God. And pray in the Spirit on all occasions with all kinds of prayers and requests. With this in mind, be alert and always keep on praying for all the saints."

"things." We can become so enamored with the opportunities and challenges and pleasures of life that we begin focusing on ourselves rather than on why Christ left us on earth!

All Christians need to evaluate their priorities in life constantly. Let us not be lulled to sleep and become like the majority of the people around us. Our eyes need to be wide open.

Be Self-Controlled (v. 6b, 8)

With the exhortation to be self-controlled, Paul was warning the Thessalonian Christians that it is possible to lose self-control. We must continually put on the "full armor of God" (Eph. 6:11). Be assured that if there is a chink in our armor—as individuals or as a church—Satan will make his move.

In verse 8, Paul uses another illustration. He contrasts a state of self-control with a state of drunkenness. First he wrote, "For those who sleep, sleep at night, and those who get drunk, get drunk at night" (v. 7). To be drunk is to be controlled and unable to respond as we should. An underlying thought here is that there are certain kinds of conduct that are acceptable to the sons of darkness but unacceptable to the sons of light. Conduct of this sort has no place in the lives of believers, for we "belong to the day" (v. 8).

Then Paul outlines how to be self-controlled in verse 8. First, put on the breastplate of faith and love. Faith in God protects inwardly, and love for people protects outwardly.

Next, put on the helmet of the hope of salvation, which guards the head from attacks on our thinking.

▶ **15. Read Ephesians 6:11–18 (in the margin). Compare the pieces of armor found in 1 Thessalonians 5 with those listed in that chapter.**

_____
_____
_____

Encourage One Another (v. 11)

Being alert and self-controlled is a process we cannot achieve by ourselves. We need encouragement from other believers. Knowing this truth makes it all the more important that we "not give up meeting together, as some are in the habit of doing, but let us encourage one another—and all the more as you see the Day [of the Lord] approaching" (Heb. 10:25).

The longer we live, the more diligent we should be about meeting with other Christians to "build each other up" in our faith, in our hope, and in our love (v. 11). One of the first things that can happen in our world of abundant opportunities and competitive activities is to neglect the important personal and family function of attending church regularly. And when we do, we begin to lose our cutting edge as Christians. We can be lulled to sleep.

▶ **16. Sometimes we think to encourage others only in times of difficulty or sorrow. Encouragement, according to this passage, needs to be given to the spiritual edification of others. List some specific things that can be spiritually encouraging.**

_____

_____

_____

There are many ways to encourage one another. First, do you know someone who used to be active as a Christian, attending church regularly and functioning as a part of the Body of Christ, but no longer is? Would you prayerfully approach that person immediately and lovingly share with him the need to be with God's people on a regular basis?

Do not feel you are imposing. Even if people do not respond, in their hearts they will appreciate your concern. Eventually they may respond. Don't let Satan intimidate you. Remember also that people may reject you outwardly but may be inwardly crying for help. Though their initial message may be mixed and confusing, they usually want someone to show concern.

One final challenge is this—are you personally ready for Christ's return? More specifically, do you know Jesus Christ personally? If not, receive Him today and you will never need to fear the Day of the Lord.

▶ **17. Consider once more this very important question: Are you ready for Jesus to return?**

Continual Growth

The Christian faith is never static, and the New Testament pictures the Christian way as one of continual growth. Those who are in Christ are growing in spiritual stature and in the knowledge and love of God (see 2 Peter 3:18 in the margin). As we study the Word of God we gain knowledge, but it is knowledge we must put into practice. Regarding this lesson, for example, we must never permit the study of prophecy

2 Peter 3:18

"But grow in the grace and knowledge of our Lord and Savior Jesus Christ. To him be glory both now and forever! Amen."

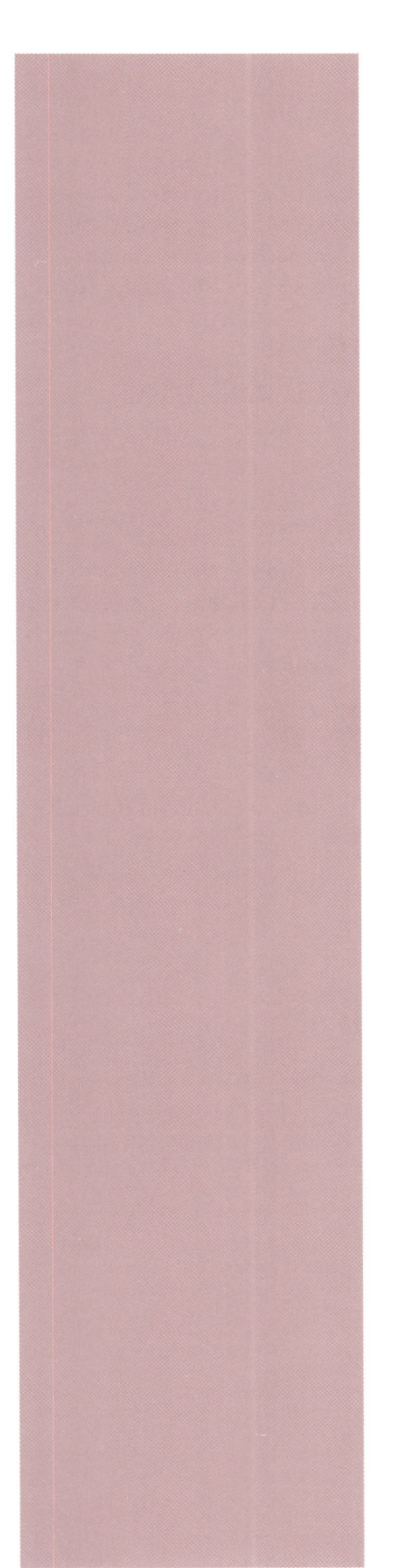

to become purely academic or a source of tension or argument.

With the study of prophecy, it seems that some people are always interested in the newest interpretation or latest view or some spectacular fulfillment. Believers don't need to hear a new interpretation of Scripture; instead, we need to remind ourselves of what we already know so that we do not forget it.

Paul has given us prophetic truth, which we need to learn. He also has given us specific instruction, which we need to follow so that what we learn affects how we live. Don't walk in your sleep, be alert, be self-controlled, and encourage others—until Jesus comes.

Small-Group Meeting 6

Opening Prayer

Begin your meeting with prayer. Thank God that He is the Sovereign of all things. Ask Him to help you live out that truth, trusting Him in every circumstance and looking forward eagerly to His return. Perhaps God will use this lesson to strengthen some in your group who are going through difficulties by reminding them that Jesus is coming soon.

Building Relationships

Allow time for each member to share one thing for which they praise God.

Reviewing the Lesson

1. Read aloud the opening story that Chuck Swindoll tells about working in a machine shop. Ask, "Do you think Christians today live as if Jesus could come any minute?"

2. What are some prophetic events that people mistakenly think must take place before the Rapture? (Keep in mind that often these are actually signs of the Second Coming. The Bible does not mention any signs that must precede the Rapture. See Lesson 5, Part 3 on page 63 to review the distinction between the Rapture and the Second Coming.)

3. Why are "thief in the night" and "labor pains" good metaphors for Paul to use in this chapter?

4. Part 4 (pp. 76ff) emphasizes how these truths should affect the way we live. Discuss each of the actions we are encouraged to take. Lead the group in thinking about very specific things they should do to be alert, to be self-controlled, to put on the breastplate of faith and love, and to put on the helmet of the hope of salvation.

Applying the Truths to Life

Select interactive questions to discuss as a group. Be careful to choose ones that are for open discussion, since some are intended for personal reflection only. Include some from each of the four parts of the lesson. Significant questions to consider from this lesson include #1 (p. 70), #7 (p. 71), #11 (p. 74), #12 (p. 74), and #15 (p. 77).

Now go back over the actions listed in Part 4. Ask if each one is clear to every member of the group.

Ministering to One Another

One of the ways we can minister to others is to help each live a godly, pure life. Talk about the need to be accountable to one another. Encourage all to develop an accountability relationship.

Reaching Out to Others

Now would be a good time to talk about multiplying by dividing. Perhaps some from your group would take this study material and lead another group through it. Take what you have learned from this experience and share it with others.

Closing Prayer Time

Share prayer requests that have been answered and submit new ones. Spend time praying that God will help each in the group to have a repentant heart. Pray, by God's grace, that each member of the group will be ready to meet Jesus.

LESSON 7

Leadership and Partnership

1 Thessalonians 5:12–15

Say the word *pastor* and what comes to mind? An "Ann Landers" column summed up a popular viewpoint of the typical pastor.

"Results of a computerized survey indicate that the perfect pastor preaches exactly 15 minutes. He condemns sin, but never embarrasses anyone. He works from 8:00 a.m. until midnight and is also the janitor.

"He makes $60 a week, wears good clothes, drives a new car and gives $50 a week to the poor. He is 28 years old, has been preaching for 25 years, is wonderfully gentle and handsome, loves to work with teenagers and spends countless hours with senior citizens. He makes 15 calls daily on church families, shut-ins and hospital patients, and is always in his office when needed.

"If your pastor does not measure up, simply send this letter to six other churches that are tired of their pastors, too. Then, bundle up your pastor and send him to the church at the top of the list. In one week you will receive 1,643 pastors. One of them should be perfect."

Now, say the word *pastor* again and what comes to mind?

"He has the strength of an ox, the tenacity of a bulldog, the daring of a lion, the wisdom of an owl, the harmlessness of a dove, the industry of a beaver, the gentleness of a sheep, the versatility of a chameleon, the vision of an eagle, the hide of a rhinoceros, the perspective of a giraffe, the endurance of a camel, the bounce of a kangaroo, the stomach of a horse, the disposition of an angel, the loyalty of an apostle, the faithfulness of a prophet, the tenderness of a shepherd, the fervency of an evangelist, the devotion of a mother."[1]

Someone has suggested five ways to get rid of your pastor:

1. Sit up front, smile, and say "amen" every time he says something good. He will preach himself to death.

2. Pat him on the back and tell him what good work he is doing in the church and community. He will work himself to death.

3. Increase your offering to the church. He will go into shock.

4. Tell him you've decided to join the visitation group and win souls for the Lord. He will probably suffer a heart attack.

5. Get the whole church to band together and pray for him. He will get so efficient that some other church will hear about him and give him a call. That will take him off your hands.

These are just a few of the many humorous descriptions of pastors and their relationship with their churches. Though said with tongue in cheek, they focus on an important subject—roles and relationships in the church, particularly those between the congregation and its leader. This is not a new subject. From the first-century church until now, the subject of relationships in the church has always been discussed. Paul does that here in this section of 1 Thessalonians as he writes about leadership and partnership: how we are to relate to the leaders of the church and to one another.

▶ **1. Before beginning this lesson, write down the name of your pastor(s) and other leaders in your congregation. Then pray that God will help you learn from this lesson the principles that will enhance your relationship with and support for these leaders.**

_____
_____
_____

PART 1: Interacting with the Scripture

Reading/Hearing God's Word

Read or Listen to:

☐ 1 Thessalonians 5:12–15

▶ **2. Using your Bible, read or listen to the passage of Scripture listed in the margin. As you begin, ask God to speak to you through His Word. Watch for verses or ideas that are especially meaningful to you today. Once you finish, check the box indicating that you have read the passage.**

Meditating on God's Word

▶ **3. Write a brief summary of a meaningful verse or idea you noticed.**

_____
_____
_____

LESSON 7: LEADERSHIP AND PARTNERSHIP

> **1 Thessalonians 5:12–15**
>
> ¹² "Now we ask you, brothers, to respect those who work hard among you, who are over you in the Lord and who admonish you. ¹³ Hold them in the highest regard in love because of their work. Live in peace with each other. ¹⁴ And we urge you, brothers, warn those who are idle, encourage the timid, help the weak, be patient with everyone. ¹⁵ Make sure that nobody pays back wrong for wrong, but always try to be kind to each other and to everyone else."

Memorizing God's Word

▶ 4. During the time you are studying this lesson, commit to memory 1 Thessalonians 5:15. Memorizing this key verse will help you remember the important features of this lesson.

Understanding God's Word

▶ 5. Read again the focal passage for this week's lesson (1 Thess. 5:12–15) in the margin. Underline any key phrases or ideas that seem especially meaningful to you.

▶ 6. Look back at these verses. Circle one of the underlined phrases or words that you would like to understand or experience more fully.

Looking through the Scripture to God

Now pause to pray: "Lord, I thank You for my church, where You have placed godly leaders to help me with my spiritual journey. And I thank You for others in the Body of Christ with whom I travel in this journey. Help me know better my responsibilities toward these leaders and fellow travelers."

PART 2: The Responsibilities of Leaders (5:12–13)

Paul did not refer to the spiritual leaders in the church either by name or title. He was probably writing about elders, since these were the first leadership positions filled in New Testament churches. As Paul and Barnabas traveled together establishing churches in various cities on their first missionary journey, they eventually retraced their steps and "appointed elders for them in each church" (Acts 14:23). Since the church in Thessalonica was relatively new at the time Paul wrote his first letter to them, we can assume these were the men he had in mind.

On the other hand, it's possible that leaders had emerged in the church who had not been officially appointed. This, of course, happens in any social organization. There are those who are more highly motivated and put in a great deal of time and effort to their service. Perhaps this is why Paul first identified these leaders as "those who work hard among you." Such people are leaders not in name only, but in their actions as well. Three different leaders are mentioned in verses 12–13.

The words Paul used to describe the leaders of the church tell us much about what is expected of those who serve in leadership roles.

Being a leader is not just a matter of being chosen and given a title—it is a working responsibility. Paul described the leaders with the following words and phrases.

▶ **7. Make a list of the areas of responsibilities in your church. Your list may include such things as music, Sunday school, or maintenance. This will remind you that there are many jobs to do at church and many workers needed to do them.**

_____

_____

_____

Those Who Worked Hard among Them (v. 12)

These leaders worked. The implication of the Greek words used here is that their efforts were strenuous, resulting in weariness. Add to that the fact that these men probably were not "vocational" ministers—this was not their job. They were not paid but gave of themselves freely, with great effort in service to the church.

▶ **8. If you are a worker in your church, you know that your labor can be hard, wearying work. You appreciate acts of encouragement directed to you. Now, think of someone in your church whom you can encourage and write down what you will do, such as writing a thank-you note or giving some baked goods to that person.**

_____

_____

_____

Those Who Were Over Them in the Lord (v. 12)

This statement implies these leaders were recognized as having authority in the church. They were decision-makers. If they were officially elders, their authority was understandable, for this was their God-ordained task. They were to be overseers and managers. They were to "take care of God's church" (see 1 Timothy 3:1–5 in the margin). This is why elsewhere in Scripture they were alluded to as shepherds or pastors (Acts 20:29; 1 Pet. 5:2). They held positions of spiritual leadership in the church and were responsible to God for those under their care (see Hebrews 13:17 in the margin).

---

1 Timothy 3:1–5

"Here is a trustworthy saying: If anyone sets his heart on being an overseer, he desires a noble task. Now the overseer must be above reproach, the husband of but one wife, temperate, self-controlled, respectable, hospitable, able to teach, not given to drunkenness, not violent but gentle, not quarrelsome, not a lover of money. He must manage his own family well and see that his children obey him with proper respect. (If anyone does not know how to manage his own family, how can he take care of God's church?)"

Hebrews 13:17

"Obey your leaders and submit to their authority. They keep watch over you as men who must give an account."

► **9. Sometimes the most difficult position in a church is that of a follower. Has a decision ever been made that everyone agreed with enthusiastically? More often decisions bring disagreement. What are some specific things you can do to help maintain the unity in the church when decisions are not unanimous?**

_____
_____
_____

Those Who Admonished Them (v. 12)

The Greek word Paul used here, which is translated "admonish," is a very strong word. It literally means to warn people who are involved in doing things that violate the will of God. To admonish means to "put in mind to obey." When Paul met with the Ephesian elders, he used this word to describe his dealings with those who "distort the truth" (Acts 20:30).

Paul was dealing with a special need in Thessalonica. Evidently, Timothy reported that some of these Christians were resisting the warnings being issued by their spiritual leaders. When the Word of God cuts across areas in our life that are out of harmony with God's will, it is painful. Either we will respond to the truth in obedience or we will reject the truth. And sometimes, in rejecting the truth, we also reject those who teach the truth.

► **10. It is easier to talk about someone than it is to talk to someone. Why do we typically struggle to admonish others?**

_____
_____
_____

PART 3: Our Attitudes toward Leaders (5:12–13)

Paul gave the believers in Thessalonica three basic exhortations regarding their attitudes and actions toward their spiritual leaders. Their attitudes would affect their actions and benefit the church as a whole.

Respect Your Leaders (v. 12)

The concept Paul expressed here is rather specific. It literally means "to know the worth" of these leaders or to "appreciate the value" of their efforts. If these leaders were truly serving the people, as they evidently were, and working very hard in the process, then they were to be highly valued and respected—not rejected, criticized, or ignored.

There are various ways, of course, that God's people can express this attitude. One is tangibly described in Paul's first letter to Timothy, who was appointing spiritual leaders in the church in Ephesus. Paul wrote, "The elders who direct the affairs of the church well are worthy of double honor, especially those whose work is preaching and teaching" (1 Tim. 5:17). The words *double honor* refer to financial remuneration. Paul is telling us to take care of the material needs of those who give themselves primarily to ministry.

▶ **11. Write down what you value about the leaders of your church. If your list is short, perhaps the problem is with your respect. Read again what *respect* means and consider how well you are obeying this instruction.**

_____

_____

_____

But taking care of a spiritual leader's material needs is not the only way to tangibly express respect. In fact, in many churches there are elders and other special leaders who are not staff members. They serve as lay leaders and devote hours of time and energy in carrying out their ministry to people. These spiritual leaders do not expect financial remuneration. But they should be honored—in some cases more than those staff pastors who are remunerated. They not only spend hours on the job every day making a living, but they also spend long hours ministering to people's spiritual needs in the church. Every Christian should honor and respect these people. They deserve words of praise and thanks!

Esteem Your Leaders (v. 13)

The second attitude we should demonstrate toward our spiritual leaders is esteem. The Greek word used here means to hold them in the highest regard. In a sense it is synonymous with an attitude of respect, yet there is more to it. Esteem is a continual attitude of affection. We are to hold leaders in the highest regard in love. Then, Paul added that if for no personal reason, we should esteem our leaders for their work. Spiritual leaders are not perfect. They make mistakes. But they should be esteemed nevertheless because of the very nature of the "work" they do.

LESSON 7: LEADERSHIP AND PARTNERSHIP

▶ 12. What are common ways of showing disrespect to church leaders? Why are church leaders such easy targets for criticism?

___

___

___

Hebrews 13:17

"Obey your leaders and submit to their authority. They keep watch over you as men who must give an account. Obey them so that their work will be a joy, not a burden, for that would be of no advantage to you."

It is easy to criticize, compare, and have extremely high expectations of our leaders. When we disagree with the leaders of our church, we must handle those disagreements in a biblical, God-honoring way (see Hebrews 13:17 in the margin).

Live in Peace with Each Other (v. 13)

The next exhortation is a command, one that is the result of the first two exhortations. As a command it is an imperative, something that must be done. There must be peace in the church. Much of the dissension that wreaks havoc in a church is traceable to church members disobeying these first two exhortations. A church will lack unity when its leaders do not lead or when the body does not permit its leaders to lead.

Conversely, those who are in positions of responsibility must keep in mind that leadership is not dictatorship. Leaders set the example; they pay the price by laboring hard and seeking to help others in Christian love. In contrast, a dictator uses law, not love; drives and does not lead; and is motivated by selfish gains, not by that which is for the good of the church.

It is not enough to have church leadership; there must also be partnership, with each member doing his share of the work. In urging the Thessalonians to show respect for their leaders, Paul was thinking especially about the disorderly persons who made this admonition necessary. Therefore it is not surprising that the next instruction begins with a warning to those who were affecting the harmony of the body.

PART 4: Our Responsibilities toward Each Other (5:14–15)

Paul spoke next about the responsibilities that all members of the local Christian body have toward each other. Spiritual leaders are responsible to give overall guidance to the church and to take a lead role in shepherding and teaching. But every believer is responsible to assist in carrying out the same basic functions, working together for the welfare of the congregation. The congregation as a whole has the shared responsibility of admonishing the disorderly, encouraging the timid, and helping the weak in faith.

The six commands Paul issued in verses 14–15 are continuous responsibilities we have to one another.

Warn Those Who Are Idle (v. 14)

Idleness was a particular problem in the Thessalonian church. Some believers were not working. Consequently, they became "busybodies" and evidently got into all kinds of trouble (see 2 Thessalonians 3:14 in the margin).

Though it is difficult to do, sometimes the most effective exhortation comes from a very close friend and brother or sister in Christ. Those who are "out of line" need to be warned.

▶ 13. How are idleness and gossip related?

_____
_____
_____

Encourage the Timid (v. 14)

In most churches there are far more people who need to be encouraged than is sometimes realized. They are the timid, or as the Greek word in verse 14 means, "little souls." They do not need criticism. They lack courage and emotional strength. They need a helping hand, a kind word, a pleasant smile, and a warm touch. They need someone to say, "I'm your friend! I really care!" These fainthearted people tend to become discouraged and despondent more easily than most. They need cheering up, stimulation to press on, and extra help to live the Christian life. They are to be helped, not rejected, by the strong.

The verb *encourage* is a combination of the words meaning "near" and "speech." Instead of scolding from a distance, get close and speak tenderly to help make them stronger in the faith.

Help the Weak (v. 14)

Paul is speaking primarily of those who are struggling spiritually when he says to "help the weak." These are the people who have difficulty living the Christian life. The temptations to sin seem more than they can bear.

---

2 Thessalonians 3:14

"If anyone does not obey our instruction in this letter, take special note of him. Do not associate with him, in order that he may feel ashamed."

Helping one another is one reason why groups such as Alcoholics Anonymous have been so effective. These people help each other. They model victory. And they are available to each other—to listen and to encourage—when the temptation to fall becomes overwhelming.

Should this not be true—and even more so—in the church? If this is going to happen, each and every one of us in the Body of Christ must participate. After all, it is only those who know us well who can discern when we're struggling.

▶ **14. Both the "little souls" and the weak need encouragement. Think about a particular situation where you could be an encouragement, as an individual or as a group. Then decide a course of action, thinking through exactly what you will do. Finally, set the plan in motion—get it done.**

_____

_____

_____

Galatians 5:22–23

"The fruit of the Spirit is love, joy, peace, patience, kindness, goodness, faithfulness, gentleness and self-control. Against such things there is no law."

Romans 12:17, 19, 21

"Do not repay anyone evil for evil. Be careful to do what is right in the eyes of everybody. . . . Do not take revenge, my friends, but leave room for God's wrath, for it is written: 'It is mine to avenge; I will repay.' . . . Do not be overcome by evil, but overcome evil with good."

Be Patient with Everyone (v. 14)

Patience is a great virtue. It is the opposite of being short-tempered. If we're going to "encourage the timid" and "help the weak," it will take patience. People generally do not change their ways overnight. It can be tough to be patient, but we must. The fruit of the Spirit includes patience (see Galatians 5:22–23 in the margin). God expects it of us and the Holy Spirit equips us for it. What remains is the developing of our patience.

Make Sure that Nobody Repays Wrong for Wrong (v. 15)

This injunction is most difficult to apply. Our natural tendency is to say, "If you hurt me, I'll hurt you. I'll get even!" Perhaps revenge was going on in the Thessalonian church. Paul had instructed them to warn the idle. A person rebuked can become a person who retaliates.

The wrong reaction of others is not a reason for us to do wrong. This does not mean that we should not confront or deal with the sinful actions against us. But we must follow God's procedure. And personal retaliation is never His plan. Paul made this clear in Romans 12 (see Romans 12:17, 19, 21 in the margin).

▶ **15. How do you feel when confronted? Does Satan use those feelings to tempt you to retaliation?**

_____

_____

_____

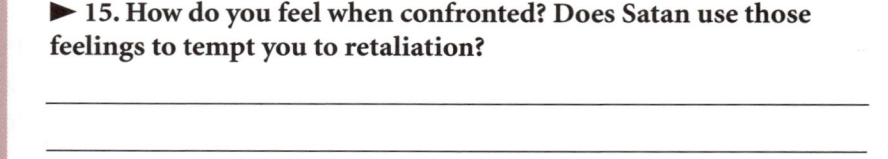

Retaliation is not an option for a Christian. We are not to be like the person who was once bitten by a rabid dog. He rushed to the hospital and called for his doctor. The doctor entered the emergency room and found the man writing feverishly on a pad of paper. The doctor said he didn't think the dog bite would be fatal, so there was no immediate need for a will. "Oh, this isn't a will, Doctor," the man said. "I'm just making a list of people I want to bite."

Always Try to Be Kind to Each Other and Everyone Else (v. 15)

This is an extension of Paul's exhortation not to pay back "wrong for wrong." Jesus even included our enemies in this group. Speaking to the crowds on a mountainside one day, He said, "You have heard that it was said, 'Love your neighbor and hate your enemy.' But I tell you: Love your enemies and pray for those who persecute you" (Matt. 5:43–44). This is a positive command, one that necessitates action. It is not enough just to abstain from evil (to not hate); we must also do good, that which is beneficial to others (love and pray for our enemies).

In the cartoon "Dennis the Menace," Joey and Dennis are pictured leaving the Wilsons' house with cookies in hand. What Dennis says to Joey exemplifies the spirit of this instruction: "Mrs. Wilson gives you a cookie because she is nice, not because you're nice."

Both parts of this passage (1 Thess. 5:12–15) are vital for a church to be the kind of church God wants. A church in which there exists a commitment to and a practice of biblical leadership and partnership will stand out as a bright testimony for the truth of God's Word. Too many people have a wrong impression of the church. Their opinion may have come from hearing about or experiencing the kind of severe disagreement that can split a church. Or perhaps their impression is that the church is always asking for money and is never involved in genuine ministry in the lives of people.

A local church moves forward in this backward-moving world by committing to biblical leadership and partnership.

Small-Group Meeting 7

Opening Prayer

Begin your meeting with prayer. This lesson has special application to us as individual members of the Body of Christ who participate in a local church. Ask God to help you consider your role in the church as you relate to the leaders He has given, and as you worship and serve in a community of believers.

Building Relationships

Allow time for each member to tell how being a part of the church is a blessing.

Reviewing the Lesson

1. It has been said that humor is only the truth thinly veiled. As you read the humorous descriptions of pastors in the opening section, do you see how the truth is thinly veiled? In particular, these paragraphs point to the unrealistic expectations of parishioners. Ask the group to discuss some of the unrealistic expectations people have about their pastors and how those can hurt the church.

2. Review the three basic exhortations Paul gave in 1 Thessalonians 5:12–13. When they are clearly understood, discuss concrete ways to show respect, esteem others, and live in peace.

3. Read aloud the first paragraph of Part 4 (p. 87), which points to the responsibility of confronting the disorderly in the church. Then read the following sentence aloud and ask the group to comment on it: "It is easier to talk about someone than to talk to them."

4. The exhortations in Part 4 include two that are very personal: the need for patience and to not be vengeful. In what ways are impatience and revenge related? Similarly, how can patience help a person control the impulse to retaliate?

5. Summarize this lesson with four specific action steps, two that you will take toward leaders and two that you will take toward others in the congregation.

Applying the Truths to Life

Select interactive questions to discuss as a group. Be careful to choose ones that are for open discussion, since some are intended for personal reflection and are not for sharing with the group. Include some from each of the four parts of the lesson. Significant questions to consider from this lesson include #1 (p. 82), #7 (p. 84), #11 (p. 86), #12 (p. 87), #13 (p. 88), and #15 (p. 90).

Ministering to One Another

Look over the specific exhortations in Part 3 and Part 4. Select one that you will make every effort to live out this week. Write an action plan in the margin of your study guide. Share it with others in the group, and plan to be held accountable at your next group meeting.

Reaching Out to Others

Continue to talk about multiplying by dividing. See if some are willing to form a new group, one that invites others to participate in this study. A second time through the study will aid them in learning the material, and leading others through will benefit them as well.

Closing Prayer Time

Share prayer requests that have been answered and mention new ones. Conclude the study time by praying that God will help you live a life committed to the community of believers, both in attitude and actions toward leaders and in partnership with others.

LESSON 8

Departing from the Norm

1 Thessalonians 5:16–28

Someone once formulated "The Seven Wonders of the Word." They are:

1. The wonder of its formation—the way in which it grew—one of the mysteries of time.

2. The wonder of its unification—a library of 66 books, yet one Book.

3. The wonder of its age—the most ancient of all books.

4. The wonder of its sales—the bestseller of all time.

5. The wonder of its interest—the only book in the world read by all classes of people.

6. The wonder of its language—written largely by uneducated men, yet the best book from a literary standpoint.

7. The wonder of its preservation—the most hated of all books, yet it continues to exist.

Paul's first letter to the Thessalonians confirms these statements. As he concluded this epistle, giving some final instructions to these relatively new believers, we see once again the wonder of Scripture. Paul concisely outlines 11 power-packed exhortations and injunctions, each one worthy of a complete chapter. Space prohibits our doing that, so let's look at each one briefly.

PART 1: Interacting with the Scripture

Reading/Hearing God's Word

▶ **1. Using your Bible, read or listen to the passage of Scripture listed in the margin. As you begin, ask God to speak to you through His Word. Watch for verses or ideas that are especially meaningful to you today. Once you finish, check the box indicating that you have read the passage.**

Read or Listen to:

☐ 1 Thessalonians 5:16–28

Meditating on God's Word

▶ **2. Write a brief summary of a meaningful verse or idea you noticed.**

_____

_____

_____

Memorizing God's Word

▶ **3. During the time you are studying this lesson, commit to memory 1 Thessalonians 5:23 (in the margin). Memorizing this key verse will help you remember the important features of this lesson.**

Understanding God's Word

▶ **4. Read again the focal passage for this week's lesson (1 Thess. 5:16–22) in the margin. Underline any key phrases or ideas that seem especially meaningful to you.**

▶ **5. Look back at these verses. Circle one of the underlined phrases or words that you would like to understand or experience more fully.**

Looking through the Scripture to God

Now pause to pray: "Father, as I come to the close of this book, may its challenges continue to motivate me as I live in fellowship with others in the Body of Christ. May our church be strengthened, our leaders encouraged, our relationships enhanced, and our faith reinforced by these truths."

1 Thessalonians 5:23

"May God himself, the God of peace, sanctify you through and through. May your whole spirit, soul and body be kept blameless at the coming of our Lord Jesus Christ."

1 Thessalonians 5:16–22

"Be joyful always; pray continually; give thanks in all circumstances, for this is God's will for you in Christ Jesus.

"Do not put out the Spirit's fire; do not treat prophecies with contempt. Test everything. Hold on to the good. Avoid every kind of evil."

PART 2: Three Unusual Exhortations (5:16–18)

These three exhortations are unusual because they are unique to Christianity. In fact, apart from Christian theology, they don't make sense. They are considered illogical and irrational by the average person, and certainly not realistic. Let's look at each one individually and see why each is so unusual.

Be Joyful Always (v. 16)

"How is it possible to be joyful always?" you ask. Certainly this is a logical question. To comprehend what Paul meant when he commanded us to "be joyful always," we need to understand that he was not talking about joy in the usual sense. He was not referring to a consistent emotional high. It is impossible and unrealistic to live on that plane. Furthermore, that kind of living would be harmful to us physically, since it is abnormal. God did not design the human body to tolerate excessive amounts of adrenalin being released into our physiological system—a phenomenon that invariably happens when we are experiencing unusual emotional excitement on a prolonged basis.

▶ **6. Remind yourself again of the difference between happiness and joy. Write a few sentences stating that.**

_____

_____

_____

Emotions fluctuate not only because of difficult situations, but also due to physical drain that accompanies the normal responsibilities of life. So Paul refers not to some euphoric state, but to an unusual sense of contentment and inner peace that every Christian can experience in spite of life's circumstances, inner turmoil, grief, stress, or even physical pain.

Paul testified to this reality in his own life in his second letter to the Corinthians. After outlining a series of incredible personal experiences—"troubles, hardships and distresses; in beatings, imprisonments and riots; in hard work, sleepless nights and hunger" (2 Cor. 6:4–5)—he concluded his description with an amazing statement. We are "sorrowful," he wrote, "yet always rejoicing" (v. 10).

This does not mean that a joyful response was automatic with Paul, nor does it mean it is automatic for any Christian. Writing to the Philippians from a Roman prison, Paul stated, "I have learned the secret of being content in any and every situation, whether well fed or hungry, whether living in plenty or in want." The secret? "I can do everything through him who gives me strength," he exclaimed (Phil. 4:12–13). When facing circumstances that were at times unbearable and beyond his control, Paul drew inner strength from Jesus Christ.

To be "joyful always" is a supernatural experience that results when we look to God for help, see the good that can result from the experience, and look beyond the present pain to envision the maturity that will result from particularly difficult situations. James had this perspective in mind when he wrote, "Consider it pure joy, my brothers, whenever you face trials of many kinds, because you know that the testing of your faith develops perseverance. Perseverance must finish its work so that you may be mature and complete, not lacking anything" (James 1:2–4).

▶ **7. What are four specific actions you can take to maintain joy in a time of pain?**

_____

_____

_____

_____

Pray Continually (v. 17)

When Paul told the Thessalonians to "pray continually," he was not instructing these Christians to spend 24 hours a day talking to God. Rather, he was implying that it is possible to be in a constant spirit of prayer. Our thoughts and concerns can be so focused on God that every desire of our heart is consistently in harmony with His will. Our very thoughts become prayer.

▶ **8. Do you have a plan for praying? If not, make one. Decide on a time of day and a place, and have a prayer list. Now write down the time and place. Ask others about how they maintain their prayer lists. You may learn about an effective way to keep track of requests and answers.**

_____

_____

_____

Being in a spirit of prayer does not mean that we must constantly be sober and somber. Even laughter and humor can be a setting in which our hearts are in tune with God. The very week I (Gene) wrote this chapter I was ministering to a group of pastors on the West Coast. Just before I spoke one evening, four of these men did a humorous takeoff on preachers. I haven't laughed that hard for a long time. It was fun laughing at ourselves. As I stood up to speak, I could only thank God in my prayer before the message for the proverb, "A cheerful heart is good medicine" (Prov. 17:22).

Paul was making another point when he exhorted believers to "pray continually." He was simply saying, "Don't forget to pray on a regular basis. Make it a priority in your life."

A mind-set of continuous prayer enables us to receive inner strength and to be able to rejoice in the midst of difficult situations. Paul clearly integrated joy and prayer in his letter to the Philippians. Note how the two elements are blended in this passage.

> Rejoice in the Lord always. I will say it again: Rejoice! Let your gentleness be evident to all. The Lord is near. Do not be anxious about anything, but in everything, by prayer and petition, with thanksgiving, present your requests to God. And the peace of God, which transcends all understanding, will guard your hearts and your minds in Christ Jesus (Phil. 4:4–7).

"That sounds great!" you're tempted to say. "But, could Paul really practice this in his own life?"

Luke records an event that illustrates this experience not only in Paul's life but also in that of his missionary companion Silas. Both were thrown in prison in Philippi, where the Christians lived who received the Philippian letter. These missionaries had been severely beaten and locked up in the inner cell, the place reserved for hardened criminals. Their feet were fastened in stocks. In that setting, with blood still oozing from their wounds, they lifted their voices to God. "About midnight Paul and Silas were praying and singing hymns to God" (Acts 16:25).

Paul did practice what he preached. He had learned the "secret of being content" in all circumstances.

▶ **9. Are you genuinely thankful for your circumstances? How can focusing on your circumstances keep you from being thankful, and how can focusing on God help you be thankful? Consider which you are doing.**

_____

_____

_____

Give Thanks in All Circumstances (v. 18)

I (Gene) had the privilege of writing an article for *Decision* magazine entitled, "You Don't Have to Be Afraid of a Nuclear Holocaust." In that article I made reference to Paul's statement that we are to "give thanks in all circumstances." I further explained that to "give thanks in all circumstances" does not mean that a Christian has to give thanks *for* all circumstances.

I received a letter from a dear woman who read the article. Referring to Paul's statement in 1 Thessalonians, she wrote, "This truth has been a mainstay in my life. I was married to a blind man for almost 34 years. During that time, we pastored churches until eight months before his death at 69—over 30 years. Ten years ago he passed away, and especially since that time I have aimed to thank God 'for' and 'in' those circumstances."

This woman's response indicates that there's a very fine line between thanking God *in* all circumstances and *for* all circumstances. When we thank God in our circumstances, our focus is on knowing that He is ultimately in control and that He will help us through them. To thank Him for the circumstances is an attitude of submission that acknowledges that even the most difficult times can be for our benefit.

There are some things that happen that we don't believe God wants us to thank Him for. If we did, we would be thanking Him for evil. However, He always wants us to be thankful in the midst of any situation—thankful that He is in control of our lives, that He is with us, that He will never forsake us.

▶ **10. In your own words, state the difference between being thankful "in" and "for" your circumstances. Then determine to be both.**

_____

_____

_____

Paul culminates these three injunctions with the following statement: "For this is God's will for you in Christ Jesus" (v. 18). Thus, these three unusual exhortations are not just Paul's desire for us, but they are God's will for us.

PART 3: Five Cautions (5:19–24)

In this next section, Paul outlines five succinct cautions for the Thessalonian Christians. In order to understand his concern, we need to look at all of these in concert:

- "Do not put out the Spirit's fire" (v. 19).

- "Do not treat prophecies with contempt" (v. 20).

- "Test everything" (v. 21).

- "Hold onto the good" (v. 21).

- "Avoid every kind of evil" (v. 22)

Lesson 8: Departing from the Norm

One of the ways God communicated with New Testament believers was by the gift of prophecy. For example, when Paul was on his way to Jerusalem he stayed at Philip's house in Caesarea. Luke records that "a prophet named Agabus came down from Judea." In order to communicate a message he had received from God, "he took Paul's belt, tied his own hands and feet with it and said, 'The Holy Spirit says, "In this way the Jews of Jerusalem will bind the owner of this belt and will hand him over to the Gentiles"'" (Acts 21:10–11).

This, of course, was a correct message. It happened as Agabus said it would. A true prophet was enabled by the Holy Spirit to predict the future with total and absolute accuracy. In fact, this was the test of a true prophet in the Old Testament. To claim falsely to be a prophet in Israel was punishable by death (see Deuteronomy 18:20–22 in the margin).

As in the days of the Old Testament, there were those in the New Testament who claimed to have the gift of prophecy and to receive messages from God. But they were not true prophets. Their messages were not authentic. But since this gift existed, Paul warned these Christians not to stand in the way of what the Holy Spirit wanted to communicate through a particular member of the church. They were not to have a negative attitude toward prophetic messages.

However, Paul warned them to test what was communicated very carefully and to respond only to that which was good. In saying that, Paul put forth the possibility that there are those who speak so-called messages from God who are not good. Rather, they are evil. In fact, they could be inspired by Satan.

> **Deuteronomy 18:20–22**
>
> "'A prophet who presumes to speak in my name anything I have not commanded him to say, or a prophet who speaks in the name of other gods, must be put to death.'
>
> "You may say to yourselves, 'How can we know when a message has not been spoken by the LORD?' If what a prophet proclaims in the name of the LORD does not take place or come true, that is a message the LORD has not spoken. That prophet has spoken presumptuously. Do not be afraid of him."

▶ **11. How does your knowledge of the Bible help you to discern things you hear others say are "from God"?**

_____
_____
_____

This raises a very important question. Is this gift of prophecy operative today? Bible teachers disagree on this issue. Some of us believe that this gift was operative primarily during the first century while Christianity was becoming established and the New Testament Scriptures were coming into existence. However, we must remember that God can do anything He wants at any moment in history. Thus, Paul's cautions to the Thessalonian Christians are still applicable today.

Some of what is practiced today does not have the ring of authenticity when compared with the prophecies that took place in the New Testament, when this gift was exercised. Today, a so-called prophecy is often just a repetition of Scripture or is so general in nature that what is predicted does indeed come to pass—and most people know from experience what is going to happen anyway. Perhaps you have noticed that tabloid newspapers have "prophecies" in them at the beginning of each year. Some of the predictions can be quite vague, leaving ample room for the predictions to "come true." Likewise, some of the so-called prophecies that Christians give today can be quite vague. To say, "God is going to answer that prayer you have been praying," or, "An unexpected blessing will come into your life," can give people hope. These statements are general enough and are likely to happen anyway. They should not be considered as an authentic word from God.

It is also easy to be self-deceived in these areas. Some people sincerely claim to have this gift and say that their message is one they have received directly from God. Perhaps their study of Scripture has convinced them that they are so gifted, or perhaps a person will take what was a New Testament gift and in their confusion simulate that gift in his own mind.

We must compare the practices and beliefs of people with the Word of God. The Bible is the objective standard by which all behavior and beliefs are to be judged. In light of this, we must be careful students of the Bible, allowing the Word to speak, to say what it says, and not finding what we want in the Bible or manipulating its teaching to fit our beliefs.

▶ **12. Read 1 Corinthians 14:13–35. Look for "rules" Paul gave to the church to regulate the exercise of spiritual gifts in worship services. List the specific rules, such as, "There must be an interpretation given." These will help you recognize that many of the practices we may see today break the rules.**

_____
_____
_____
_____
_____

Paul's concern is that we must be very cautious about listening to people who claim to have a message from God. We must "test everything" very carefully, but at the same time be very careful that we do not interfere with the work of God's Holy Spirit—to "put out the Spirit's fire" (v. 19).

A Prayer for Total Sanctification (vv. 23–24)

It is not accidental or surprising that Paul follows these cautions about prophecy with a prayer for growth and maturity. This is the emphasis of the New Testament. Nowhere are we, as individuals, told to seek for or to attempt to discover our spiritual gifts. Rather, we are told again and again to become mature in Jesus Christ. This is what Paul means here by "sanctification": "May God himself, the God of peace, sanctify you through and through. May your whole spirit, soul and body be kept blameless at the coming of our Lord Jesus Christ. The one who calls you is faithful and he will do it" (vv. 23–24).

The Thessalonian Christians were well on their way toward Christian maturity—both corporately and personally. This is one reason why Paul began his letter by thanking God for their "work produced by faith," their "labor prompted by love," and their "endurance inspired by hope" (1:2–3). As mentioned in Lesson 1, when Paul wrote a letter to a church he was pleased with in terms of its spiritual growth, he would often begin by thanking God for these three qualities in that particular church.

▶ **13. In your own words, define what it means for a person to be holy.**

_____

_____

_____

PART 4: Some Concluding Injunctions (5:25–28)

The three injunctions at the end of this letter are not particularly related. One is a personal prayer request. Another emphasizes the importance of demonstrating affection and love to each other, and the third is an exhortation to these believers to share the message of this letter with all the Christians in Thessalonica and the surrounding area.

Pray for Us (v. 25)

Paul seldom focused on his own needs. However, he always acknowledged his need for prayer. And often his prayer request focused on the need to be faithful to the Lord in sharing the Gospel. For example, in writing to the Ephesians, he requested, "Pray also for me, that whenever I open my mouth, words may be given me so that I will fearlessly make known the mystery of the gospel, for which I am an ambassador in chains. Pray that I may declare it fearlessly, as I should" (Eph. 6:19–20).

▶ **14. Share with others—and learn from them—how to have a prayer list. At the top of your prayer list, write out 1 Thessalonians 5:25.**

Greet All the Brothers with a Holy Kiss (v. 26)

This is one of five such exhortations in the New Testament (see also Romans 16:16, 1 Corinthians 16:20, 2 Corinthians 13:12, and 1 Peter 5:14). The important issue in this exhortation is not the form of the greeting but the meaning behind it. The way in which people express love and affection varies from culture to culture. But whatever that greeting, it should always be a meaningful, holy expression.

▶ **15. Is your church a friendly church? Remember, *you* are the church. After church this week, write down the name of someone you greeted. Then write down the name of someone you greeted whom you usually do not. Special assignment: write down the name of a visitor you met.**

_____

_____

_____

I (Gene) remember one occasion when I walked into a church and greeted a young high school student named Bruce. I asked him how he was doing. About a minute later, one of the elders tapped me on the shoulder and told me he wanted to admonish me in love. He had overheard my greeting to this young man.

"What did I do?" I responded.

He reviewed the scenario for me. "You asked Bruce how he was doing," the man said. "But you did not stay around long enough to hear his answer."

At this point, of course, this elder had my undivided attention. "What did he say?" I asked.

"Well," he replied, "when you asked him how he was doing, he responded by saying, 'Not very well. My brother was in a motorcycle accident today.'"

My heart sank. I realized that in my busyness and preoccupation with other things, I had asked him how he was doing but was merely exercising a ritualistic greeting. I had not really intended in my heart to find out the answer to that question. I'm thankful that a sensitive elder overheard the conversation and admonished me so that I could go back and ask forgiveness. The young man readily forgave me.

▶ **16. Have you ever said, "I'll pray for you" and then forgotten to do it? Go back to your prayer list. Learn to write down every need brought to your attention.**

When we greet people, we should do so sincerely. We should avoid getting caught in meaningless protocol. Christians of all people should be sincerely interested in one another and express that interest in a culturally acceptable way.

▶ **17. After you have prayed for a special request, ask that person what God has been doing in regard to that request.**

Have This Letter Read to All the Brothers (v. 27)

Remember the "Seven Wonders of the Word" from the introduction to this lesson, the seven qualities that make Scripture unique? Verse 27 gives us a glimpse into that uniqueness. Though 1 Thessalonians was indeed written first and foremost to the Thessalonians, it is a part of God's Holy Word. Consequently, it is just as relevant today as it was during the first century. As pastors and teachers, may we not neglect sharing the contents of this letter with our congregations. And as individual Christians, may we not neglect to read it personally and apply its truths to our own lives.

A Final Benediction (v. 28)

After telling the Thessalonians to "have this letter read to all the brothers," Paul gives his final benediction: "The grace of our Lord Jesus Christ be with you" (v. 28). This, too, should be our prayer for others, that the grace of our Lord Jesus Christ be with them.

Small-Group Meeting 8

Opening Prayer

Begin your meeting with prayer. Thank God for the time you have had to work through this study guide and to learn lessons from 1 Thessalonians that will help you in your walk with God personally and corporately. Then ask God to help you "depart from the norm," living out the truths taught in the concluding verses of this book.

Building Relationships

Remember your determination to hold one another accountable? (Review the Ministering to One Another section from Small-Group Meeting 7.) Those actions, if followed through, help build relationships. So, now is the time for an accountability check-up.

Reviewing the Lesson

1. List the 11 power-packed exhortations and injunctions found in 1 Thessalonians 5:16–28.

2. These exhortations are grouped under three headings. If you do not get all eleven covered in one session, try to do all that are in a particular section. If you are doing the entire lesson in one session, pick at least one exhortation from each section and give it special attention. If you try to cover all 11, the discussion may bog down and seem like "exhortation overload." Be sensitive to the needs and interest levels of your group.

3. In Part 4, the concluding injunctions include greeting one another with a "holy kiss" (p. 102), meaning a sincere greeting. Read aloud those paragraphs. What are ways in which we insincerely greet one another?

Applying the Truths to Life

Select interactive questions to discuss as a group. Be careful to choose ones that are for open discussion, since some are intended for personal reflection and are not for sharing with the group. Include some from each of the four parts of the lesson. Significant questions to consider from this lesson include #7 (p. 96), #10 (p. 98), #13 (p. 101), and #14 (p. 102).

Ministering to One Another

The concluding exhortations of 1 Thessalonians 5 direct your attention to the needs of others. Look over them and decide how you can incorporate each of them into your life or improve on what you are already doing.

Reaching Out to Others

If you have chosen to start a new group, make it happen! Plan the first session, draw up a list of people to contact, decide who will do what—and get it done.

Closing Prayer Time

Share prayer requests that have been answered while the group has met and prayed. Pray that God will help each in the group to apply the truths learned from this study so that they will be more like Christ, and that your church will see and experience the blessing of people who want to live God's way in this world. Also, pray for the new group of people who will be studying this material, if applicable.

Notes

Lesson 1

[1] Woodrow Kroll, *Back to the Bible: Turning Your Life Around with God's Word* (Portland, Oreg.: Multnomah Publishers Inc., 1999), p. 80.

[2] David W. Henderson, *Culture Shift* (Grand Rapids, Mich.: Baker Books, 1998), pp. 97–98.

[3] Gary W. Demarest, *The Communicator's Commentary Series, Vol. 9* (Dallas, Tex.: Word, Inc., 1984), p. 27.

Lesson 2

[1] *The Disciple's Study Bible* (Nashville, Tenn.: Holman Bible Publishers, 1988), p. 1535.

Lesson 4

[1] Warren Wiersbe, *The Bible Exposition Commentary, Vol. 2* (Wheaton, Ill.: Victor Books, 1989), pp. 175–176.

[2] Mort Katz, *Living Together* (Rockville Centre, N.Y.: Farnsworth Publishing Co., 1982).

Lesson 5

[1] John MacArthur, *First Corinthians* (Chicago: Moody Press, 1984), pp. 441-442.

[2] Michael W. Holmes, *The NIV Application Commentary: 1 and 2 Thessalonians* (Grand Rapids, Mich.: Zondervan Publishing House, 1998), p. 157.

[3] Quoted by Susan Bergman, "In the Shadow of the Martyrs," *Christianity Today*, August 12, 1996, p. 25.

[4] William J. Gaither. "Because He Lives," *Worship His Majesty* (Alexandria, Ind.: Gaither Music Company, 1987), #260.

Lesson 6

[1] Charles Swindoll, *Rise & Shine* (Portland, Oreg.: Multnomah Press, 1989), pp. 167–169.

[2] Warren Wiersbe, *The Bible Exposition Commentary, Vol. 2* (Wheaton, Ill.: Victor Books, 1989), p. 183.

[3] Michael W. Holmes, *The NIV Application Commentary: 1 and 2 Thessalonians* (Grand Rapids, Mich.: Zondervan Publishing House, 1998), pp. 166-167.

[4] Ibid., pp. 175–176.

Lesson 7

[1] As quoted in Richard W. DeHaan, *Your Pastor and You* (Grand Rapids, Mich.: Radio Bible Class, 1979), pp. 12–13.

Interacting with God
Small–Group Covenant

Believing that God wants His people to be a healthy Body of Christ with Jesus Christ Himself as its Head, we submit ourselves to Him and to one another so that we may help one another grow into mature believers and so that, as a group, we "may be built up until we all reach unity in the faith and in the knowledge of the Son of God and become mature, attaining to the whole measure of the fullness of Christ" (Eph. 4:12-13). Together we agree to:

1. Study God's Word each week and complete the learning activities for the week's lesson prior to the group meeting.

2. Pray regularly and specifically for one another, our church, our spiritual leaders, and those who need to come into a saving relationship with Jesus Christ.

3. Attend all group meetings unless unavoidable circumstances prevent attendance. If we are unable to attend, we will make every effort to notify our group leader and let him know how the group can pray for us in our absence.

4. Participate in the meetings by listening carefully and sharing openly.

5. Keep confidential any personal matters discussed by other members during the meetings.

6. Seek to demonstrate love as the Holy Spirit leads us to help meet one another's needs.

7. Seek to bring glory and honor to God through our relationships with one another.

Signatures: **Date:** _____